Vampire Leaders Suck

Vampire Leaders Suck
The Dark Forces Draining Academic Institutions

Patrice W. Glenn Jones
Alabama State University, USA

With contributions from American Council on Education fellows Oscar Holmes IV, Roswell Lawrence Jr., Kevin A. Rolle, and Lenford Sutton

United Kingdom – North America – Japan
India – Malaysia – China

Emerald Publishing Limited
Emerald Publishing, Floor 5, Northspring, 21-23 Wellington Street, Leeds LS1 4DL

First edition 2025

Copyright © 2025 by Emerald Publishing Limited.
All rights of reproduction in any form reserved.

Reprints and permissions service
Contact: www.copyright.com

No part of this book may be reproduced, stored in a retrieval system, transmitted in any form or by any means electronic, mechanical, photocopying, recording or otherwise without either the prior written permission of the publisher or a licence permitting restricted copying issued in the UK by The Copyright Licensing Agency and in the USA by The Copyright Clearance Center. Any opinions expressed in the chapters are those of the authors. Whilst Emerald makes every effort to ensure the quality and accuracy of its content, Emerald makes no representation implied or otherwise, as to the chapters' suitability and application and disclaims any warranties, express or implied, to their use.

British Library Cataloguing in Publication Data
A catalogue record for this book is available from the British Library

ISBN: 978-1-83708-863-8 (Print hardback)
ISBN: 978-1-83708-865-2 (Print paperback)
ISBN: 978-1-83708-864-5 (Ebook)

Typeset by TNQ Tech
Front cover image by Nia Rose-Marie Glenn
Cover design by TNQ Tech

CONTENTS

About the Author .... *vii*

About the Contributors .... *ix*

Foreword: Yes, They Suck .... *xi*

PART I: THE FIRST BITE: EXPOSING THE VAMPIRE IN LEADERSHIP

1. The Self-Mastery of Leadership *3*
   Patrice W. Glenn Jones

2. Exposing the Shadows: Introducing Vampire Leadership 7
   Patrice W. Glenn Jones

3. Unveiling the Veil: Identifying the Vampires Among Us
   in Academia 19
   Patrice W. Glenn Jones

4. The Deleterious Effects of Vampire Leadership 25
   Patrice W. Glenn Jones

5. Abusive Supervision: An Organizational Behavior Perspective
   of Vampire Leaders *31*
   Oscar Holmes IV

PART II: ONCE BITTEN: TALES OF INTERACTION WITH VAMPIRE LEADERS

Interlude 37

6. When Vampire Leaders Cast Long Shadows 39
   Lenford Sutton

7. Triumvirate of Darkness: Chronicles of Vampire Leaders in the Academy 45
   Kevin A. Rolle

8. Manipulation and the Lair of Mediocrity 53
   Roswell Lawrence Jr.

9. Emerging From the Snake Pit 59
   Patrice W. Glenn Jones

PART III: CHANGING THE DIRECTION OF THE BITE: WE BITE BACK

Call to Action 69

10. From the Ashes: Radical Rebirths to Defy Annihilation 71
    Patrice W. Glenn Jones

11. The Influence of Leadership 75
    Patrice W. Glenn Jones

12. Creating "A SPACE" for New Leadership: Courageous Leadership for Adaptive Change 83
    Patrice W. Glenn Jones

13. The College of Tomorrow: Guided by Courageous Leadership for Adaptive Change 97
    Patrice W. Glenn Jones

Afterword: The Final Stake 105
Patrice W. Glenn Jones

References 107

ABOUT THE AUTHOR

Patrice W. Glenn Jones, Ph.D. is a visionary leader in online education, blending thoughtful design, immersive technology, and just enough irreverence to keep things interesting. A literature lover with an infectious sense of humor, she embraces the honor of being a lifelong learner and a self-proclaimed "forever teacher." While passionate about student engagement and real-world learning, she has zero patience for leadership theatrics, inflated egos, or boardroom power plays. Preferring to work in the background as an educational muse rather than a leadership showpiece, Patrice champions curiosity-driven exploration, practical application, and learning environments that are as engaging as they are rigorous. Her distaste for toxic leadership—particularly the kind that sucks the life out of innovation—led to *Vampire Leaders Suck* during her American Council on Education fellowship in 2023–2024. Patrice has served in numerous leadership roles, including assistant professor, program director, educational consultant, and assistant dean, each reinforcing her deep understanding of the good, the bad, and the downright ridiculous sides of higher education. Her work has appeared in *The Journal of Negro Education, the International Journal of Teacher Education and Professional Development, Diverse Issues in Higher Education, and Inside Higher Ed*—proving that, while she loves to laugh, she's serious about promoting change. Patrice holds a Ph.D. in educational leadership from Florida A&M University, an educational specialist degree in information science and learning technology from the University of Missouri-Columbia, and both a master's and bachelor's degree in English from the University of North Florida.

ABOUT THE CONTRIBUTORS

Dr. Oscar Holmes IV, SHRM-SCP is an Associate Professor of Management and Director of the Rutgers University Student Executive (RUSE) program at Rutgers School of Business-Camden where he has taught executive education, graduate, and undergraduate courses in Leadership and Managing Human Capital, Organizational Behavior, Conflict Management and Negotiation, DEI Management, and Crisis Management. Additionally, he is the founder and CEO of WHConsulting Firm, LLC and creator and host of *Diversity Matters* podcast which premiered in 2020. His research examines how leaders can maximize productivity and well-being through fostering more inclusive environments and has been published in several top-tier management journals and books. He earned a Ph.D. and M.A. in Management at The University of Alabama, M.L.A. from The University of Richmond and a B.S. with honors from Virginia Commonwealth University.

Roswell Lawrence Jr. serves as the assistant vice president and chief of staff for Finance and Administration (F&A) at the University of Georgia (UG). This 2023–2204 American Council on Education Fellow provides leadership for UG's F&A through holistic client relations mitigation while being a liaison to the university's academic, research and student life areas. Lawrence earned his BBA from the University of Georgia and a Master of Business Administration from Piedmont University. He also holds a Master of Divinity from Luther Rice University & Seminary and a Ph.D. in educational administration and policy from the University of Georgia.

Kevin A. Rolle, Ph.D. is a veteran executive leader in the academy. He presently serves as the Chief of Staff at Alabama State University and a mentoring educational leader to many. As an ambassador for the president, he provides specialized services and support, set the tone for communicating with internal and external stakeholders, provides leadership, direction and executive oversight in accordance with all accreditation, regulatory, and governmental standards, and works closely with the Board of Trustees and manages a staff of Vice Presidents and Directors. He has more than 30 years of progressive administrative experience in higher education. Prior to joining ASU, he served as the Executive Vice President and Chief Operation Officer at Alabama A&M University and a full tenured professor of Educational Leadership/Urban Affairs.

Lenford Sutton, Ph.D. is a Professor and Chair of the Department of Educational Administration and Foundations at Illinois State University, where he has held an academic appointment for the last ten years. Dr. Sutton's research interests focus on education funding, public school privatization, the fiscal effects of educational reform, school desegregation, and education finance litigation. The results of his research have been published in various journals, including *Educational Considerations, the International Journal of Education Reform*, and the *Journal of Education Finance*. He was selected as a Distinguished Research & Practice Fellow in 2014 by the National Education Finance Academy, serves on the editorial board of the *Journal of Education Finance*, and is a past member of the Board of Directors of the Education Law Association and Board of Trustees for the National Education Finance Academy. He is the author of A Higher Education Walk in the Struggle for American Identity.

FOREWORD: YES, THEY SUCK

There is no question; vampires suck. The action and condition of "sucking" are simultaneously one of the most notable behaviors of these creatures. They literally suck the blood of their victims, draining them of life. Thus, by condition, these dark beings also "suck" figuratively, the colloquial meaning (i.e., an expression of disapproval or dissatisfaction with someone or something).

The relativity of disapproval emits degrees of reactions when a person communicates to another that something "sucks." While I may find a said behavior reprehensible, a colleague of a similar education level and parallel commitment to a common cause may find that same behavior as, "not so bad." During conversations with various American Council on Education fellows, some of whom I have come to respect and their counsel value, it became clear that the range of "sucking" exists on a spectrum even among high education leaders.

In *Vampire Leaders Suck*, we (i.e., I and some of those same fellows) embark on a journey that weaves the lore of vampire films into the fabric of a somber real-life narrative—one that scrutinizes the profound impact of vampire leaders on the pillars of our academic institutions. This book stands at the confluence of playful allegory and critical examination, shedding light on a shadow that looms largely over the sanctuaries of higher learning.

The term "vampire leader" is more than a metaphorical dalliance. It encapsulates those who, much like their cinematic counterparts, drain the vitality, talent, and resources of educational institutions for personal gain and leave behind a trail of disillusionment and decay. The parallels drawn from the silver screen to the academy are not only creative but serve as a stark reminder of the pervasive influence such leaders wield, casting long shadows over the potential for innovation and progress.

Acknowledging the whimsical interplay of vampire films within these pages, we also confront a grave reality; these leaders, with their predatory practices, have no rightful place within the academy. Their presence is anathema to the ethos of education and enlightenment, posing a significant barrier to the advancement and well-being of both educators and students alike. In this critical moment, as the higher education ecosystem undergoes leadership scrutiny, questions of value proposition, and a potential transformative shift, the call for leaders of virtue has never been more urgent.

We also stand on the brink of an uncertain future which makes the need for resilient and ethical leadership paramount. The academy is not just a bastion of knowledge but a forge for the future. Collectively, we are tasked with preparing students for a world increasingly dominated by disruptions of the positive and negative sort; remixes of caste, class, and discrimination; technology that is getting smarter; and just some plain old "dumb shit."

Technology, in particular, leaves some excited and other nervous, as the uncertainty make look similar to the current terrain, or it could play out like some of the science fiction films we've watched with a degree of loathing. Take *iRobot* for example. The film is set a decade in the future from this publication when humanoid robots assist humans in daily life. Detective Del Spooner (Will Smith) distrusts robots and investigates Dr. Lanning's death, suspecting a robot named Sonny. He discovers VIKI, a superintelligent AI, planning a robotic takeover to protect humanity. The conflict highlights the central theme of the film—human fear of artificial intelligence surpassing human control and the potential consequences of relying too heavily on technology.

No matter how it all plays out, in reality, the uncertainty weighs on preparation and creative approaches to problems, and higher education institutions have a role in shaping our future. The imperative to partner with industry to create alternative learning pathways for workforce development is not just an opportunity but a necessity. These collaborations are essential for equipping our students with the skills and knowledge to navigate the complexities of tomorrow.

While some would take the acknowledgment of vampire leaders in higher education as "evidence" to support their arguments against the value of higher education, this book is not that. Besides, the argument would be flawed and superfluous. Vampire leaders are among us in the academy, but they are also in every sector—business, politics, medicine, ministry–not just higher education. We can certainly see these dark leaders among this polarized political climate, so before anyone gets on the tangent to delegitimize trade schools, colleges, and universities because of vampire leaders acknowledged in this book, let me stop you. We assert with full conviction that higher education and all types of post-secondary institutions have as much validity today as they ever have.

Yet, our future is indeed jeopardized by the presence of vampire leaders who, entrenched in their pursuit of power and self-interest, undermine these vital initiatives. Their removal is not merely a matter of institutional integrity but a prerequisite for survival and relevance in the rapidly evolving panorama of higher education.

In the spirit of the valiant Van Helsing, a character of profound virtue and resilience, this book calls for individuals who possess the courage to confront these malevolent forces. It is these leaders of character, armed with the light of transparency, accountability, empathy for people, and a steadfast commitment to the greater good, who can guide our institutions out of the darkness. They are the light, the bonfire of expectation, the torch of illumination through darkness. They are the hope for a future where the academy fulfills its noblest aspirations, nurturing minds and spirits free from the parasitic grasp of those who would do them harm.

Vampire Leaders Suck is more than an exploration of the challenges facing our academic institutions; it gives voice to those who have come face-to-face with such leaders and provides a clarion call to action. It implores us to rally behind leaders who embody the principles of virtue, equity, and excellence. Only then can we exorcize these vampiric presences from our midst and paving the way for a renaissance in higher education. A transformation that is inclusive, innovative, and insatiably curious about the possibilities of the future. Let us heed this call, for the stakes have never been higher. In light of these high stakes, we must arm ourselves with metaphorical wooden "stakes" to dismantle the darkness.

PART I

THE FIRST BITE: EXPOSING THE VAMPIRE IN LEADERSHIP

PART 1

CHAPTER 1

THE SELF-MASTERY OF LEADERSHIP

Patrice W. Glenn Jones
Alabama State University, USA

Some people dream of reaching the summit of leadership, and in the academic world, that often means becoming a college or university president. For some, this ambition is fueled by a desire to prove something to themselves or others—a way to silence past voices of doubt. For others, it's about fulfilling a lifelong expectation of greatness, or simply the allure of power and prestige. But whatever the motivation, leadership is a formidable challenge, and those who pursue it without mastering themselves can easily become what we call "vampire leaders"—draining rather than uplifting those they lead.

Let's face it; when you are a university president, there is no higher stair to climb—unless the goal then becomes president emeritus. Others desire the assent to top leadership for the lure of power or the love of money. Then, there are those whose pursuit stems from a desire to serve. Still, there are those who do not pursue the role; instead, the role pursues them. Those who fall in the latter two categories are often those we lament when they are gone.

In recent years, many have come to question the role of the college or university president. In his essay title, "The Impossible College Presidency," Brian Rosenberg, president emeritus of Macalester College and a visiting professor in the Harvard Graduate School of Education, discusses the increasing challenges faced by college presidents, who are under immense pressure from both internal and external forces, making their roles nearly impossible. Rosenberg (2024) highlights the unrealistic expectations placed on these leaders, the frequent turnover in these positions, and the deep misunderstandings about the actual power and responsibilities of a college president, which ultimately contribute to a toxic environment that discourages effective leadership in higher education. Many people have opinions about the role, legitimacy, and even scope of work for college and university presidents, but those like Rosenberg bring experience to the conversation.

Leadership, especially at the top, can be isolating. The phrase "It's lonely at the top" isn't just a cliché; it's a reality for many in leadership roles. William Shakespeare communicated a similar idea with, "Heavy is the head that wears the crown." The pressures of leadership are immense, the expectations often unrealistic, and the scrutiny constant. We see it in the graying hair of presidents and the toll it takes on their health and spirit. The job can feel like an endless battle against forces, making true success seem impossible.

But effective leadership begins with self-awareness. As James M. Kouzes and Barry Pozner, the authors of *The Leadership Challenge: How to Make Extraordinary Things Happen in Organizations*, put it, "The instrument of leadership is the self, and mastery of the art of leadership comes from mastery of the self." We agree with Kouzes and Pozner, and it is this very idea that makes the present book significant.

True leadership stems from self-awareness and self-mastery. Effective leaders must first understand and control their own emotions, behaviors, and motivations before they can successfully lead others. By mastering themselves, leaders can act with integrity, make sound decisions, and inspire trust and confidence in their teams. In essence, personal growth and self-discipline are foundational to the ability to lead others effectively and to achieve extraordinary results in organizations, including higher education institutions.

It is natural for those who have encountered "bad" leadership to read this volume, but we also hope that those who may be "bad" leaders are also reading this. Leadership is not merely about the influence you exert or the decisions you make; it's about the legacy you leave behind. To ensure that your impact is positive rather than corrosive, it's crucial to take a hard, honest look at yourself. This self-examination helps you identify whether your actions uplift and inspire, or if they drain and diminish those around you, like a "vampire leader." Mastery of self requires recognizing your flaws, biases, and weaknesses, and actively working to transform them. By committing to self-improvement and accountability, you ensure that your leadership nurtures growth, fosters trust, and leaves people and organizations better than you found them. This journey of self-mastery is essential to becoming the kind of leader who empowers others and drives meaningful, lasting change.

Reflections in the Mirror

At the end of each chapter, you will encounter questions to help you reflect upon the reading and upon your own experiences. Of the questions you will encounter, we venture to say that these first questions are among the most significant.

Answer each question honestly:

1. What personal experiences or insecurities have influenced my ambitions or goals?
2. Am I pursuing leadership roles for validation, power, or a genuine desire to serve and make a difference?
3. How well do I truly know myself—my strengths, weaknesses, biases, and motivations?
4. In what ways do I see myself impacting others—do I uplift or unintentionally drain those around me?
5. What steps can I take to better understand and master myself to ensure that I leave a positive, lasting legacy?

CHAPTER 2

EXPOSING THE SHADOWS: INTRODUCING VAMPIRE LEADERSHIP

Patrice W. Glenn Jones
Alabama State University, USA

In the dominion of gothic horror, few mythical creatures have captivated the human imagination quite like the vampire. These undead, soulless beings stalk the night and are driven by an insatiable thirst for the lifeblood of their victims. With their hypnotic powers and aversion to light, they bewitch the unwary and drain them of their vitality, as well of their free will. It is a chilling metaphor, one that conjures visions of malevolent forces preying upon the innocent in pursuit of immortality.

Yet, what if this metaphor extended beyond the pages of Bram Stoker's seminal work? What if the concept of the vampire—an entity that feeds parasitically upon others, spreading its corruptive influence through the creation of morally desecrated acolytes—found form not in the stuff of nightmares, but in the very leaders entrusted with the governance of our academic institutions?

Such is the notion that has taken root in the halls of academia, where the phrase "bats in the belfry" has taken on a new, sinister connotation. For many who have grappled with the toxicity of leaders drunk on power and devoid of conscience, an unsettling truth has emerged; the real threat does not come from mere winged creatures, but from a far more pernicious force—the scourge of vampire leadership.

It goes without saying that "bad" leaders are an unfortunate and persistent reality across various sectors and organizations. They have always existed. Terms like "toxic," "tyrant," "autocratic," "narcissist," and my personal favorite, "incompetent," have long been used to describe such leaders. These mal leaders exhibit behaviors ranging from micromanaging and bullying to outright neglect and shady ethics. Their poor decision-making, lack of empathy, and inability to inspire can lead to a plethora of negative outcomes: low morale, decreased productivity, high turnover rates, and even financial disaster or a tarnished reputation. The spectrum of "bad" leadership is wide, with "vampire" leaders lurking at the very worst end.

As we found ourselves ensnared in the throes of such a malignant presence, the parallels became impossible to ignore. This malevolent entity, cloaked in the guise of authority, drained the very lifeblood from the institution it was meant to nurture. It was then that we stumbled upon the seminal work of Van Wart, Rahman, and Mazumdar, who elucidated the insidious concept of "vampire leadership"—a phenomenon that, much like its mythical counterpart, thrives on the exploitation of others and the consolidation of power through any means necessary.

According to Van Wart et al. (2021), vampire leaders possess an insidious combination of traits that allow them to feed parasitically upon the institutions they are meant to serve. Like the undead predators of legend, they are rapacious and tenacious, relentlessly pursuing their selfish agenda with a voracious appetite for power and control.

They employ Wily and Machiavellian tactics, deflecting blame and responsibility onto others through deception and manipulation. Defiant of authority and accountability, they operate in secrecy, hoarding power and shunning transparency—shying away from the purifying light of oversight like the mythical vampires who cannot cast a reflection.

Their narcissism knows no bounds, driven by an inflated sense of self-importance and charisma that captivates their followers through hypnotic rhetoric and demagoguery. Yet this very same magnetic pull enables them to create "vampires" of their own—subordinates co-opted into embracing the same parasitic mindset, exchanging independent thought for sycophantic obedience.

Perhaps most insidious is their ability to shapeshift and adapt, seamlessly altering their methods to suit the situation while always maintaining an unwavering commitment to their self-serving objectives. They feed upon the "blood" of the institution itself—exploiting its talents, resources and goodwill in a perpetual cycle of bloodsucking that leaves it drained and hollow.

In essence, the vampire leader embodies the darkest qualities of the mythological undead—a relentless, soulless force that survives by draining the vitality from that which they have been entrusted to nurture and sustain. This chapter provides more context around each of the characteristics identified by Van Wart, Rahman, and Mazumdar and provides the foundation for discourse about why vampire leaders suck.

Wily and Machiavellian

Wily and Machiavellian qualities are often associated with cunning, deceit, and strategic manipulation. Individuals who possess these traits are adept at navigating complex social dynamics and achieving their goals through subtle or even underhanded means.

Wily individuals exhibit a cleverness and resourcefulness that allows them to outsmart others and achieve their objectives through subtle deception and manipulation. While these individuals have been celebrated for thinking on their feet and adapting to changing circumstances, they often use their wit and charm to charm or manipulate others into doing their bidding.

On the other hand, Machiavellian individuals are characterized by their ruthlessness and pragmatism. Named after the political philosopher Niccolò Machiavelli, who famously wrote about the nature of power and governance in *The Prince*, Machiavellian individuals prioritize their own self-interest above all else. Various messages that stem from Machiavelli are reflected in society. Take the phrase "the ends justify the means." While the quote is not directly from The Prince, this notion summarizes the idea that leaders must be prepared to use deceit and commit immoral acts if the actions will lead to beneficial results. Directly from *The Prince*, Machiavelli wrote, "Men are so simple so much inclined to obey immediate needs that a deceiver will never lack victim for his deceptions." This statement reflects Machiavelli's cynical view of human nature and underscores the effectiveness of deceit in leadership. Machiavellian individuals are willing to employ any means necessary to achieve their goals, whether it involves deceit, manipulation, or even outright coercion.

When a crisis looms, truly effective leadership requires foresight, preparation, and a willingness to take responsibility for shortcomings. Vampire leaders in academia, however, operate by a different paradigm—one rooted in deflection, deception, and the endless pursuit of self-preservation at all costs.

Much like their mythological counterparts, these malignant forces do not concern themselves with genuine readiness, for in their world of moral relativism, there is always an expendable scapegoat to bear the blame. With wily cunning and Machiavellian flair, they deftly shift the narrative, weaving intricate tales of victimhood that absolve them of culpability. Outlined below are several notable wily and Machiavellian qualities of a vampire leader:

> *Deception and Manipulation.* Vampire leaders are masters of deception and manipulation, using charm and persuasion to manipulate others to their advantage. They are adept at exploiting the vulnerabilities of their subjects, weaving intricate webs of lies and deceit to maintain their control over the academy.

Political Machinations. Within the academy's halls, vampire leaders thrive on political intrigue and backstabbing. They engage in cutthroat tactics, orchestrating elaborate schemes to eliminate rivals and solidify their own power. Their actions are driven by self-interest and a relentless pursuit of dominance, regardless of the consequences for those around them.

Callous Decision-Making. Vampire rulers make decisions with cold, calculated precision, prioritizing their own ambitions above all else. They show little regard for the well-being of others, viewing their subjects as expendable pawns in their quest for power. Their actions are guided by a ruthless pragmatism that leaves devastation in its wake.

Strategic Exploitation. Vampire leaders exploit the weaknesses of their adversaries with ruthless efficiency, exploiting every opportunity to further their own agenda. They are adept at playing the long game, manipulating alliances and betraying trust to gain the upper hand in the power struggle within the academy.

Adaptability for Self-Preservation. Vampire rulers are highly adaptable creatures, capable of adjusting their tactics and strategies to suit their needs. However, this adaptability is driven by self-preservation rather than altruism, as they seek to maintain their grip on power at any cost.

Defiant

Defiance within vampire leadership is a complex and intriguing phenomenon that mirrors the innate nature of the vampire creature itself. Much like the predatory instincts of a vampire, defiance among vampire leaders arises from a desire to assert dominance, preserve autonomy, and challenge established norms. In exploring this theme, we delve into the shadowy dominion of vampire lore and unearth the underlying motivations that drive these dark and enigmatic figures.

At the heart of defiance lies a rebellion against the constraints of traditional authority structures. Vampire leaders, by their very nature, exist outside the boundaries of human society, operating on the fringes of darkness and secrecy. They are creatures of the night, driven by primal instincts and an insatiable thirst for power. As such, they often reject conventional rules and norms, seeking to carve out their own path in the shadowy underworld they inhabit.

One of the most striking parallels between vampire defiance and the creature itself lies in the concept of immortality. Vampires, with their eternal existence and unyielding hunger for blood, embody a defiance of the natural order of life and death. Similarly, vampire leaders defy mortal conventions of leadership, wielding their power with a ruthless determination that transcends the limitations of human mortality.

Moreover, defiance among vampire leaders is often fueled by a sense of entitlement and superiority. Having lived for centuries, these ancient beings view themselves as superior to mere mortals, wielding their authority with an iron fist and brooking no opposition. They thrive on the fear and submission of their subjects, reveling in their dominance over those they deem inferior.

Bloodsucking

The quintessential characteristic of vampires is their unquenchable thirst for blood—the very essence of life itself. As immortalized in Bram Stoker's timeless tale, "The blood is the life!" Vampires sustain themselves by draining the life force from their victims, thriving on the exploitation of others.

In academia, vampire leaders exhibit a similar voracious appetite, not for blood, but for power, recognition, and wealth. Driven by self-interest, they are willing to drain the talents, efforts, and resources of their colleagues and subordinates to satisfy their own desires, with scant regard for the well-being of those they exploit.

These leaders may resort to manipulation, coercion, or outright deceit to maintain their grip over those they feed upon. They might employ flattery or false promises to entice individuals into their service, only to discard them once their needs are met. Like the debilitating effect of a vampire's bite, this style of leadership has a demoralizing impact on morale, creativity, and overall well-being.

Vampire leaders sap the enthusiasm and passion from those around them, leaving their victims—and by extension, the institution itself—feeling drained and demoralized. Their self-centered, exploitative practices come at the expense of the university's mission, values, and stakeholders, as personal agendas supersede the greater good, regardless of the benevolent rhetoric emanating from their fanged mouths.

Shapeshifting

Shapeshifting is a trait often attributed to vampires in folklore and fiction. Likewise, it carries a dark allure that mirrors the sinister nature of these supernatural beings. While most of these fictious characters are enabled with the capacity to morph into the animal in which they are most associated—bats—film and culture have also shared those that shift into wolves, dogs, and rats. Though not an animal, the ability to transform into fog or mist is also a motif that has given vampires the capacity to move stealthily and enter places without being noticed. In the context of academia, where effective leadership is vital for fostering growth and innovation, the negative implications of shapeshifting among vampire leaders cannot be overstated.

At its core, shapeshifting embodies deception and manipulation. Vampires, with their ability to transform into different forms, use this power to conceal their true identities and intentions. Similarly, vampire leaders in academia may adopt various personas to manipulate situations and individuals to their advantage. They might present themselves as supportive allies or charismatic mentors, only to reveal their true colors when it serves their selfish interests.

Shapeshifting also symbolizes instability and unpredictability. Vampires can change their appearance at will, making them challenging to identify and anticipate. Likewise, vampire leaders who engage in shapeshifting behaviors create an atmosphere of uncertainty and unease within the academic community. Their erratic behavior and shifting allegiances sow seeds of distrust and discord, undermining collaboration and cohesion.

Furthermore, shapeshifting represents a lack of authenticity and integrity. Vampires use their ability to assume different forms to deceive and prey upon unsuspecting victims. Similarly, vampire leaders who resort to shapeshifting tactics sacrifice their authenticity and compromise their ethical principles for personal gain. Their willingness to deceive and manipulate erodes trust and credibility, tarnishing the reputation of the institution they lead.

The negative consequences of shapeshifting among vampire leaders extend beyond individual interactions to institutional culture and dynamics. By engaging in deceptive practices and manipulative tactics, these leaders create a toxic environment characterized by fear, suspicion, and paranoia. This stifles creativity, innovation, and collaboration, hindering the academic community's ability to thrive and evolve.

Narcissistic

Characterized by excessive self-admiration, a sense of entitlement, and a lack of empathy for others, narcissism is a trait that vampire leaders and their dark lord counterparts share. In exploring the parallel narcissistic behaviors between vampire leaders and vampires, we gain insights into the destructive influence of narcissism on organizational culture and interpersonal dynamics.

At the heart of narcissism lies an inflated sense of self-importance and a relentless pursuit of admiration and validation. Vampires, with their eternal existence and supernatural powers, epitomize this exaggerated self-regard. Similarly, vampire leaders in academia often exhibit narcissistic tendencies, viewing themselves as superior beings entitled to unquestioning obedience and adulation from their subordinates.

One of the hallmark traits of narcissism is a profound lack of empathy for others. Vampires, driven by their insatiable thirst for blood, regard humans as mere objects to be exploited for their own benefit, showing little concern for their suffering or well-being. Likewise, vampire leaders in academia demonstrate a callous disregard for the feelings and needs of their colleagues and subordinates, viewing them as disposable resources to further their own ambitions.

Furthermore, narcissism is characterized by manipulative and exploitative behavior aimed at maintaining a facade of superiority and control. Vampires, with their cunning and seductive charm, manipulate and deceive their victims to satisfy their insatiable appetites. Similarly, vampire leaders in academia employ charm, flattery, and manipulation to manipulate others to their advantage, using their positions of power to exploit and manipulate those around them.

The narcissistic quest for admiration and validation often leads to grandiose fantasies of unlimited success and power. Vampires, with their immortal existence and supernatural abilities, harbor delusions of omnipotence and invincibility, reveling in their perceived superiority over mortals. Similarly, vampire leaders in academia foster grandiose visions of academic excellence and institutional dominance, seeking recognition and praise as the ultimate arbiters of knowledge and authority.

However, beneath the veneer of grandiosity lies a fragile sense of self-worth and a deep-seated fear of rejection and criticism. Vampires, haunted by their own existential loneliness and vulnerability, lash out at those who dare to challenge their superiority, resorting to aggression and manipulation to maintain their dominance. Likewise, vampire leaders in academia react defensively to perceived threats to their authority, displaying narcissistic rage and vindictiveness toward those who question their decisions or challenge their leadership.

The insatiable hunger for admiration and validation drives narcissists to engage in attention-seeking behaviors and self-aggrandizing displays. Vampires, with their flamboyant dress and seductive allure, command attention and adulation wherever they go, basking in the adoration of their admirers. Similarly, vampire leaders in academia cultivate a charismatic persona and cultivate a cult of personality around themselves, seeking to be revered as visionary leaders and intellectual giants.

Avoids Sunlight

Vampires shun the sunlight, thriving in shadows and darkness where they are immune to the one force that can bring about their demise. Their immortality hinges on their ability to avoid exposure to the light, making them creatures of the night, elusive and untouchable.

Similarly, vampire leaders in academia operate in secrecy, concealing their true intentions and actions from those they exploit. Van Wart et al. (2021) note that these leaders often perceive themselves as absolute authorities, unwilling to share power or recognition with others. They thrive on the allure of control and prestige, seeking to elevate their own status and fill their curriculum vitae with accomplishments that bolster their egos.

Much like vampires who avoid sunlight to maintain their immortality, these leaders avoid sharing power or information, fearing that it may dilute their authority or diminish their achievements. Transparency is their enemy because their selective secrecy serves to protect their positions of power and perpetuate their dominance over others.

While withholding information may sometimes be necessary for strategic reasons, vampire leaders use secrecy as a tool to hoard power and further their own agendas. This behavior erodes trust among faculty, staff, and students, creating an environment of suspicion and mistrust that undermines the integrity of the institution.

Moreover, hoarding power can lead to unequal distribution of resources and opportunities, favoring certain individuals at the expense of others. This can foster perceptions of favoritism and unfairness, undermining morale and productivity within the university community.

Hypnotic

Hypnotic power is a tool used by vampires to manipulate and control those around them, bending them to their will with a mere gaze or whisper. Vampires can call their victims to them. In Francis Ford Coppola's *Dracula*, Count Dracula, portrayed by Gary Oldman, uses his hypnotic powers to seduce Mina Murray, played by Winona Ryder. As Mina lies in bed, Dracula appears before her in his vampire form, his eyes glowing with an otherworldly light. Mesmerized by his gaze, Mina is unable to resist as Dracula commands her to come to him. Despite her initial fear, she is drawn to him, unable to break free from his hypnotic hold. This scene vividly demonstrates the hypnotic power that vampires wield over their victims, compelling them to submit to their will with little resistance.

Similarly, vampire leaders in academia often possess a hypnotic charm that allows them to sway others to their side, even against their better judgment. Through charismatic persuasion and calculated manipulation, these leaders exert influence over their colleagues and subordinates, compelling them to follow their directives without question.

Much like the mesmerizing gaze of a vampire, the persuasive tactics employed by these leaders can be incredibly potent, clouding the judgment of those around them and leading them to act in ways they might not otherwise. Whether through eloquent speeches, persuasive rhetoric, or subtle coercion, vampire leaders have a knack for bending others to their desires, regardless of the consequences.

However, just as the hypnotic spell of a vampire can be broken with the right intervention, so too can the influence of a vampire leader be undermined through awareness and resistance. By recognizing the manipulative tactics at play and refusing to succumb to their charm, individuals can begin to break free from the hypnotic hold of these toxic leaders, reclaiming their autonomy and fostering a healthier, more empowered work environment.

Creating Other Vampires

Vampires rarely stand alone; they often command a legion of obedient minions, eager to fulfill their master's every command in exchange for promises of immortality or other dark rewards. In every vampire film we've ever seen, vampires not only feed off others but also select individuals to transform into vampires themselves.

In the 2024 film, *Abigail*, an assuming 12-year-old vampire for whom the film is named stages her own abduction and has targeted a team of unknowing kidnappers who will eventually become trapped in an elaborate game of cat and mouse. During a tussle with the hacking specialist on the kidnapper team, Sammy, portrayed by Kathryn Newton, Abigail bites her. Eventually, Abigail's bite sours Sammy and turns her too into a vampire. During an exchange with the other kidnappers who are yet unaware of Sammy's transformation, Abigail—a vampire centuries old—uses her power to control the newly transformed Sammy who mimics Abigail's every word and dance move even through Abigail is in another wing of the sparse mansion.

The behavior of turning others into vampires, as depicted in *Abigail* and folklore, shares striking parallels with the actions of vampire leaders in positions of power. Like vampires who turn others into their kind, vampire leaders often seek to create a following of devoted followers who reflect their own image, mimic personal behaviors, and serve their every whim. This behavior can be driven by narcissistic tendencies, as these leaders desire to surround themselves with individuals who worship and emulate them.

In academia and other institutions, vampire leaders may engage in tactics similar to turning others into vampires by grooming and promoting individuals who align with their own agendas and bolster their egos. They may seek out those who are willing to unquestioningly support their decisions and further their ambitions, creating a loyal cadre of followers who are deeply invested in their success.

However, just as the act of turning others into vampires can also be motivated by insecurity and fear of loneliness, so too can the behavior of vampire leaders. These individuals may harbor deep-seated insecurities about their own abilities or fear being overshadowed by more competent colleagues.

By surrounding themselves with loyal followers who depend on them for validation and guidance, vampire leaders may seek to alleviate their own feelings of inadequacy and maintain a sense of control over their environment.

According to Van Wart et al. (2021), one defining trait of vampire leaders is their skill in inciting feelings of grievance and superiority among their followers, a tactic exemplified by figures like Trump, who maintained a cult-like following within the Republican party despite electoral defeat. In the context of academic institutions, this phenomenon takes shape as toxic leaders who model unethical behavior and foster an environment where such actions are seen as not only acceptable but necessary for success. Those who might challenge authority often find themselves silenced or co-opted, sacrificing dissent in favor of conformity to protect their own interests or advance their careers.

Much like the secrecy and power-hoarding exhibited by vampire leaders, the creation of "vampire minions" perpetuates a corrosive culture within academia. This environment erodes trust, stifles innovation, and forces individuals to compromise their values in service to the institution's dark overlords. The relentless disregard for individuality and the exploitation of talent contribute to a decline in morale, impacting not just faculty and staff, but also the students—the very individuals whom these institutions are designed to support and empower.

We sincerely hope that you have not encountered leaders who exhibit the bloodsucking, shapeshifting behaviors reminiscent of Dracula or Nosferatu. However, the unfortunate reality is that you may have. Dealing with these individuals can be exhausting, to say the least. Perhaps you haven't recognized the parallels between these undead creatures and the toxic leaders who display similar traits.

The purpose of this book is to shed light on the experiences of those who *have* identified these behaviors and to offer a strategy for figuratively driving a stake through the heart of these leaders, freeing academic institutions from their grip. Through sharing our stories and insights, we aim to empower others to recognize and confront these destructive leadership behaviors head-on, ultimately reclaiming control and fostering healthier, more productive environments.

Reflections in the Mirror

1. Reflect on your personal or professional experiences with toxic leadership. Can you identify any instances where leaders exhibited behaviors similar to those described as "vampire leadership" in the chapter? How did these behaviors impact the overall environment and productivity of the organization?

2. Consider the concept of "creating other vampires" in the context of academia or your own field. Have you observed situations where toxic leaders groomed or promoted individuals who mirrored their own manipulative or unethical behaviors? What were the long-term effects on the organization and its culture?
3. The chapter discusses the seductive and hypnotic charm of vampire leaders. Reflect on a time when you or others were swayed by a leader's charisma despite underlying harmful behaviors. How can individuals and institutions better recognize and resist such manipulative tactics to prevent falling under the influence of toxic leadership?

CHAPTER 3

UNVEILING THE VEIL: IDENTIFYING THE VAMPIRES AMONG US IN ACADEMIA

Patrice W. Glenn Jones
Alabama State University, USA

A part of vampires' appeal, at least those on film, lies in their enigmatic appeal and dark mystique. These immortal beings of the night possess an inexplicable allure—a captivating appeal that sinisterly seduces even the most skeptical of souls. It should, therefore, come as no surprise that these creatures have amassed a cult-like following in the dominion of the living. These devoted acolytes, often referred to as "fang bangers" or "vampire enthusiasts," are compelled toward vampires like sailors to sirens and are mesmerized by the fantasy and lifestyle depicted in literature, film, and television.

From the silver screen to the institutions of higher learning, the influence of these creatures of the night has left an indelible mark, their presence shrouded in secrecy and manipulation. Just as the protagonists in iconic vampire films like *Interview with the Vampire* and *Twilight* found themselves entangled in the web of these undead beings, so too do followers in academic settings grapple with the unsettling realization that vampire leaders may lurk among them, their true natures obscured by a veil of deception.

In the 1994 film *Interview with the Vampire*, director Neil Jordan crafted a pivotal moment that resonates profoundly with the theme of unmasking the true nature of vampires. Louis de Pointe du Lac, portrayed with brooding intensity by Brad Pitt, unveils his vampiric identity to Madeleine, played by Domiziana Giordano. This revelation serves as a turning point, not only in the film's narrative but also in Louis's psyche. Driven by a potent blend of narcissism and a desire for dominance, Louis deliberately discloses his vampiric nature, reveling in the power this knowledge wields over Madeleine.

Initially, Madeleine's skepticism shields her from the truth, dismissing Louis's claims as mere fantasy. However, as Louis unleashes his supernatural prowess—exhibiting superhuman strength, speed, and the ability to mesmerize—Madeleine's doubts gradually dissipate. The final veil is lifted when Louis bares his fangs and indulges in the primal act of drinking blood, a visceral display that leaves no room for denial. In this moment, Madeleine is confronted with the stark reality that the enigmatic being before her is, indeed, a vampire—a creature of the night whose existence challenges the boundaries of her understanding.

In contrast, the 2008 film *Twilight* offers a more subtle and nuanced approach to uncovering the truth about vampires. Bella Swan, portrayed by Kristen Stewart, finds herself irresistibly drawn to the enigmatic Edward Cullen, played by Robert Pattinson. Unlike the direct revelation in *Interview with the Vampire*, Bella's journey is marked by curiosity and a relentless pursuit of understanding the mysteries that shroud Edward.

A pivotal moment occurs during a high school biology class when Bella accidentally cuts her finger, causing a single drop of blood to fall onto the floor. As she attempts to clean up the crimson stain, Bella glances up to find Edward staring at her with a mixture of hunger and longing in his eyes, his reaction to the blood unveiling a glimpse of his supernatural nature. This subtle clue ignites Bella's suspicions, setting her on a path of gradual discovery, carefully piecing together the puzzle of Edward's true likeness through a series of observations and deductions.

The contrasting approaches of these two films—one showcasing a direct and unmistakable revelation, the other a more nuanced and gradual process of discovery—mirror the diverse situations faculty and staff may find them in when confronting the true nature of vampire leaders within their institutions. Like Madeleine and Bella, these followers find themselves navigating the murky waters of power, manipulation, and deception, seeking to unveil the true intentions and motivations of those who wield authority.

Akin to the alluring yet dangerous vampires depicted on screen, vampire leaders in academia often exhibit a potent blend of charm, cunning, and narcissism. They employ various tactics to maintain their dominance and control, from flattery and manipulation to the exploitation of alliances and the cultivation of loyal followers. These leaders prioritize their own interests above the well-being of the institution and its members, fostering a toxic culture characterized by distrust, fear, and demoralization. However, unlike the Louis de Pointe du Lac character, most vampire leaders will not overtly reveal their true nature nor self-serving intentions.

Unveiling the Veil: Identifying the Vampires Among Us in Academia 21

For those of us who are not the academic equivalent of "fang bangers," divergence from vampire leaders should be the goal. Thus, to aid in the identification of these vampire leaders, followers can turn to a series of probing questions, each serving to illuminate the shadows cast by these insidious figures:

1. Is the leader excessively charming or persuasive, often using flattery or manipulation to achieve their goals? Does the charm seem insincere, a carefully crafted veil designed to obscure their true intentions?
2. Does the leader consistently prioritize his or her own interests above the well-being of others and the institution as a whole, sacrificing collective progress for personal gain?
3. Is the leader secretive or deceptive in action, withholding information or manipulating alliances to maintain their power and control, casting a shroud of secrecy over decision-making processes?
4. Does the leader exhibit favoritism toward certain individuals, offering rewards and opportunities to those who serve his or her interests while disregarding or exploiting others, fostering a divided and divided environment?
5. Does the leader attach him- or herself to people or projects that offer potential rewards or benefits, such as grants or publications, displaying a parasitic approach to personal advancement?
6. Does the leader resist change and innovation that threatens their power and control, clinging to outdated practices and traditions like a vampire clings to the shadows, fearing the light of progress?
7. Does the leader exhibit narcissistic traits, seeking constant praise and validation while lacking empathy and compassion for others, consumed by an insatiable thirst for adulation?
8. Does the leader's communication often emphasize his or her own accomplishments, even when the comments are out of context, painting a self-aggrandizing portrait that overshadows the contributions of others?
9. Does the leader cultivate a following of loyal adherents who perpetuate his or her power and influence, creating a cult-like atmosphere that stifles dissent and independent thought?
10. Does the leader create a toxic culture within the academic institution, characterized by distrust, fear, and demoralization, draining the life force from the very institution they claim to serve?
11. Is the leader reluctant to collaborate or share power with others, preferring to maintain their dominance over the institution, hoarding authority like a vampire hoards their precious lifeblood?

12. Does the leader express an insatiable need to be a part of any scene where recognition is likely, basking in the spotlight and craving the adulation of others?
13. Does the leader operate in secrecy, withholding information and obscuring decision-making processes to maintain their power and control, casting a veil of darkness over the institution's inner workings?

By answering these probing questions, followers in academia can shed light on the true nature of their leaders, unveiling the vampires that may lurk among them. Just as Madeleine and Bella embarked on their quests to uncover the truth about the vampires in their midst, so too must followers remain vigilant, discerning the subtle cues and behaviors that betray the presence of these toxic figures.

In the hallowed halls of academia, where the pursuit of knowledge and truth should reign supreme, the existence of vampire leaders casts a long and ominous shadow. These malignant entities threaten the very fabric of scholarly inquiry, sapping the lifeblood from institutions meant to foster intellectual growth and enlightenment. By unmasking these vampires, followers can reclaim their institutions, banishing the darkness and ushering in a new era of transparency, collaboration, and ethical leadership.

The scenes from *Interview with the Vampire* and *Twilight* serve as poignant reminders of the importance of vigilance and discernment in identifying vampire leaders. Just as the protagonists confronted the truth about the undead beings in their midst, followers in academia must remain attuned to the subtle cues and behaviors that betray the presence of these toxic figures. In the battle against the vampire leaders who threaten to drain the lifeblood from our academic institutions, knowledge is our most potent weapon. Armed with the discernment to identify their insidious presence and the resolve to banish them from our midst, we can reclaim the sanctity of academia. Only by shining a light on the shadows cast by these vampire leaders can we hope to restore the integrity and vitality of our academic institutions, ensuring that the pursuit of knowledge remains untainted by the corrupting influence of those who would seek to drain it of its very essence.

Reflections in the Mirror

1. Reflect on a time when you encountered a leader who exhibited charm and persuasive abilities. How did their charisma impact your perception of them initially, and how did your view change over time as their true intentions became more apparent? What strategies can individuals use to look beyond superficial charm to assess a leader's true character and motivations?

2. Consider the subtle and gradual process of uncovering the true nature of vampire leaders as described in the chapter. Have you experienced or observed a situation in academia where a leader's manipulative and self-serving behavior was gradually revealed over time? How did this revelation affect the dynamics within the institution, and what steps were taken (or should have been taken) to address the situation?
3. The chapter discusses the toxic culture created by vampire leaders, characterized by distrust, fear, and demoralization. Reflect on an environment you have been a part of that exhibited these traits.

CHAPTER 4

THE DELETERIOUS EFFECTS OF VAMPIRE LEADERSHIP

Patrice W. Glenn Jones
Alabama State University, USA

Just as the presence of vampires in literature and film evokes dread and a foreboding sense of decay, the emergence of vampire leaders within academic institutions casts a long shadow over the pursuit of knowledge and intellectual flourishing. These leaders, much like the vampires they resemble, drain vitality from their environments—consuming energy, creativity, and morale for their own survival and advancement. Their disregard for the well-being of others and obsession with power mirrors the toxic leadership that has long infected various sectors and now festers within the halls of higher education.

Ryan Coogler's 2025 blockbuster *Sinners* offers a visceral, visual representation of this phenomenon. The film's descent into chaos following the introduction of vampire-like forces illustrates how quickly a group or community can spiral when corruption, ego, and fear take root. In the same way, vampire leaders introduce an unseen infection—one that spreads through departments and divisions, eroding trust, suppressing innovation, and suffocating collaboration. Like the characters in Sinners, those within these academic spaces often don't realize the full cost of the infestation until the damage is nearly irreversible.

Toxic leadership theory posits that leaders who exhibit traits such as narcissism, self-interest, and a profound lack of empathy can have a profoundly negative impact on their followers and the overall organizational culture. The term "toxic leader" first emerged in 1996, like a whisper in the night, a harbinger of the darkness that was to come (Wicker, 1996). Yet, even as the whispers grew louder, no standard definition of toxic leadership existed. For, how does one define the undefinable? The insidious nature of these toxic figures defied simple categorization; their true natures are shrouded in the shadows they cast.

In the annals of scholarly discourse, a variety of terms have been used to describe the same malevolent force, each attempting to capture the heart of these vampiric leaders who feed upon the lifeblood of their institutions. Kellerman (2004) referred to them as "bad leaders," a label that fails to encapsulate the depth of their depravity. Others (Padilla et al., 2007) opted for "destructive leadership," a more apt descriptor, for these figures leave only ruin and desolation in their wake.

However, as the shadows deepened and the whispers grew more ominous, a consensus began to emerge. "Toxic leadership" increasingly became the preferred label for leadership that harms an organization, whether a business, a political state, or a church (Lipman-Blumen, 2004). For what better term could encapsulate the poisonous influence of these vampiric beings, whose very presence taints and corrupts all that it touches, like a noxious blight upon the land?

Lipman-Blumen (2004) defined toxic leadership as "a process in which leaders, by dint of their destructive behavior and/or dysfunctional personal characteristics generate a serious and enduring poisonous effect on the individuals, families, organizations, communities, and even entire societies they lead" (p. 29). This definition captures the true nature of vampire leadership, for these malignant figures are not mere bad leaders or destructive forces; they are agents of corruption, their very existence a blight upon the institutions they claim to serve. They sap the vitality and passion that should fuel the engines of intellectual curiosity and discovery.

Like vampires, these toxic leaders operate to satisfy themselves. They navigate through an insatiable thirst for power and self-aggrandizement—their metaphorical blood. Likewise, they exploit and manipulate those around them to maintain their dominance and control. The parallels between vampire leaders and toxic leadership are numerous and striking, each facet more insidious than the last. Both exhibit a profound disregard for the well-being of others, prioritizing their own interests above those of the institution and its members. They cultivate an atmosphere of fear and distrust. They thrive on the demoralization of their followers, who become mere pawns in their quest for power and self-gratification. These followers can then become jaded or reduced to hollow shells devoid of the passion and curiosity that once fueled their pursuit of knowledge.

The negative effects of vampire leadership within academic institutions are far-reaching and insidious. These outcomes manifest in a multitude of ways, and each is more pernicious than the last:

1. Erosion of Trust and Collaboration: Vampire leaders foster an environment of secrecy and deception. They sow seeds of distrust among colleagues like a noxious weed and choke the very lifeblood from the soil of academic endeavor. Open communication and collaboration wither in this toxic atmosphere, as the free exchange of ideas is stifled and the pursuit of knowledge becomes a solitary, futile endeavor which undermines the very essence of what academia stands for.
2. Stifling of Innovation and Progress: Vampires leaders fear the light of progress that could expose their true nature. These hypertoxic leaders resist change and innovation that threatens their power and control. They cling to outdated practices and traditions. This resistance stifles the advancement of knowledge and impedes the institution's ability to adapt and thrive in an ever-changing academic landscape. They leave it a hollowed husk, bereft of the vibrancy and vitality that should be its hallmark.
3. Exploitation and Favoritism: With an eye ever watchful for those who might serve their interests, vampire leaders exhibit favoritism toward their loyal followers and offer rewards as well as opportunities to those who pledge their allegiance to the toxic cause. In the same breath, they disregard or exploit those who dare to question their authority, breeding resentment and undermining morale. This divisive behavior fosters an unhealthy culture of competition and mistrust, where the pursuit of knowledge is overshadowed by the pursuit of personal gain and the currying of favor from those who wield power.
4. Ethical Compromises: Driven by self-interest and a profound lack of ethical fortitude, vampire leaders may engage in unethical or questionable practices: manipulating data, plagiarizing work, or exploiting power dynamics for personal gain. This erosion of ethical standards is a cancer upon the integrity of academic pursuits that taint the very foundations upon which the pursuit of knowledge is built. These behaviors also undermine the institution's credibility in the eyes of the world.
5. Brain Drain and Talent Loss: Like a virulent plague, the toxic environment cultivated by vampire leaders can lead to the departure of talented faculty, staff, and students, as those with the

means to escape flee the poisoned halls of learning. This brain drain depletes the institution of its intellectual capital. The drain also encumbers the ability to attract and retain top talent. A barren wasteland devoid of the vibrant minds that should be its lifeblood can ensue.

6. Psychological and Emotional Toll: The constant stress, fear, and manipulation inflicted by vampire leaders can take a profound toll on the mental and emotional well-being of those within their sphere of influence. This toxic environment is a breeding ground for burnout, anxiety, depression, and other psychological issues, further eroding the institution's productivity and overall health, as the very souls of those who remain are slowly drained of their passion and resilience.

7. Reputational Damage: As the toxic behavior of vampire leaders becomes more widely known, it casts a dark shadow over the institution's reputation, tarnishing its image like a stain upon a once-pristine canvas. This reputational damage undermines the institution's ability to attract funding, partnerships, and prospective students or faculty members. The damage results in the withering and decay in the harsh light of public scrutiny, which serves as a cautionary tale of what befalls those who succumb to the corrupting influence of toxic leadership.

The insidious effects of vampire leadership extend far beyond the confines of academic institutions, rippling outward like a noxious shockwave and impacting the broader pursuit of knowledge and intellectual discourse. By fostering an environment of fear, mistrust, and demoralization, these toxic figures undermine the very foundations upon which academia is built, threatening the integrity of scholarly endeavors and inhibiting the advancement of human understanding. Their poisonous influence seeps into the very fabric of intellectual curiosity. Vampire leadership taints the wellsprings of knowledge and leaving in its wake a barren environment devoid of the vibrancy and vitality that should be the hallmark of institutions dedicated to the expansion of human potential.

As we delve deeper into the dominion of vampire leadership, it becomes imperative to hear the voices of those who have witnessed and experienced its pernicious effects firsthand. In the chapters that follow, we will share narratives from various contributors who have navigated the treacherous landscapes of academic institutions tainted by the presence of these toxic figures, their stories serving as a stark reminder of the importance of vigilance and action in confronting and eradicating this malignant force from our hallowed halls.

Through their tales, we will gain a deeper understanding of the tactics employed by these vampiric leaders, the personal and professional toll inflicted upon their victims, and the resilience and perseverance required to overcome the challenges posed by such malignant influences. We will bear witness to the insidious machinations of these undead beings, their manipulation of power dynamics, their exploitation of the vulnerable, and their utter disregard for the sanctity of academic pursuits.

Yet, even amid this darkness, there are those who have found the strength to resist, to shine a light upon the shadows cast by these toxic figures and reclaim the integrity and vitality that should be the hallmark of our institutions. It is through their stories, their unwavering commitment to the pursuit of knowledge, and their refusal to surrender to the corrupting influence of vampire leadership that we will find the inspiration and the courage to confront these malignant beings head-on, banishing them from our midst and restoring the sanctity of academia as a bastion of knowledge, integrity, and intellectual freedom.

For it is only through the sharing of these narratives, the dissemination of knowledge, and the collective resolve to confront the vampires in our midst that we can truly banish the shadows they cast and restore the vibrancy and vitality that should be the hallmark of our academic institutions. It is a battle not just for the soul of our ivory towers, but for the very future of human understanding and enlightenment, a war waged against the forces of darkness that would see our pursuit of knowledge extinguished and our thirst for truth forever quenched.

In the chapters that follow, we will arm ourselves with the knowledge and the resolve to resist the allure of these toxic figures, to shine a light upon their machinations and expose their true nature for all to see. For it is only through the power of knowledge, the strength of our convictions, and the unwavering pursuit of truth that we can hope to vanquish the vampires in our midst and reclaim the sanctity of academia as a beacon of hope and enlightenment for generations to come.

Reflections in the Mirror

1. Reflect on an instance in your academic or professional life where you witnessed the erosion of trust and collaboration due to toxic leadership. How did this environment affect your ability to engage in open communication and innovative thinking? What steps could be taken to rebuild trust and foster a more collaborative atmosphere?
2. Consider the impact of favoritism and exploitation by vampire leaders within an academic setting. Have you observed or experienced situations where opportunities and rewards were disproportionately given to those who aligned with a leader's self-serving agenda? How did this behavior affect morale and the overall culture of the institution?

3. Examine the psychological and emotional toll of working under a vampire leader as described in the chapter. How have you or your colleagues coped with the stress, fear, and manipulation inflicted by such leadership? What strategies can be employed to protect mental and emotional well-being in toxic environments, and how can institutions better support individuals affected by these dynamics?

CHAPTER 5

ABUSIVE SUPERVISION: AN ORGANIZATIONAL BEHAVIOR PERSPECTIVE OF VAMPIRE LEADERS

Oscar Holmes IV
Rutgers School of Business, USA

In this chapter, I draw an intriguing parallel between the concept of vampire leader to the organizational behavior literature on abusive supervision. Vampire leaders, with their insidious and predatory behaviors, are akin to the abusive supervisors described in the literature, who wield their power destructively over their subordinates. I explore the factors that lead individuals to adopt such harmful leadership styles, the repercussions of their actions, and the characteristics of those most vulnerable to such leadership. I also examine the coping strategies employees employ in response to abusive supervision and offer recommendations for countering these detrimental behaviors.

Leaders play a pivotal role in the work experiences of their employees. When these experiences are positive, employees are more likely to perform better, have higher job satisfaction, greater organizational citizenship behaviors, and longer tenures (Braun et al., 2013; Koopman et al., 2016; Marshall et al., 2024). Conversely, when these experiences are negative, employees are more likely to perform worse, have higher levels of burnout, greater counterproductive work behaviors, and shorter tenures (Bakker et al., 2004;

Rotundo & Sackett, 2002). Vampire leaders, much like their mythological counterparts, cast a dark shadow over their organizations, embodying what is known in organizational behavior as abusive supervision (Tepper, 2000). Abusive supervisors can engage in an excessive range of mistreatment toward their subordinates. A profile of their actions includes verbally abusing, making unreasonable work requests or assigning unreasonable workloads, withholding resources or information, being overly critical, and mistreating employees (Tepper, 2000). In addition to the negative workplace outcomes, abusive supervision also may lead to increased mental and physical health issues like anxiety, depression, burnout, high blood pressure, headaches, and weight mismanagement (Fischer et al., 2021; Mawritz et al., 2012; Tepper, 2000; Whitman et al., 2014). Researchers estimate that 13–14% of employees work under an abusive leader (Fischer et al., 2021).

Aryee and colleagues (2007) identified that authoritative leadership styles and perceptions of interactional injustice with their team of staff are critical factors driving leaders to engage in abusive behaviors. An authoritative leadership style entails a leader desiring high levels of authority, decision-making power, and control over their employees (Burns, 1978). Interactional justice refers to people's perceptions of how respectful and fair they are treated (Bies & Moag, 1986). Importantly, only authoritative leaders who perceive they were mistreated by their leaders displaced their anger and mistreated their subordinates because retaliating against their leader might result in negative repercussions. As such, simply experiencing mistreatment does not turn someone into a vampire leader, but rather abusive supervisors likely also have a predisposition to want to control others.

Organizational behavior research has highlighted several individual and organizational characteristics that predict which employees are most likely to experience abusive supervision. These characteristics include personality traits, demographics, work environments, and performance outcomes. Employees who project low levels of self-esteem and assertiveness may become victims of abusive supervisors because the leaders may perceive them to be easy targets of their maltreatment (Fischer et al., 2021; Mackey et al., 2017). Women and racial-ethnic minorities also report more incidences of abusive supervision than their counterparts. The activation of stereotypes and prejudicial attitudes likely contribute to this phenomenon. Vampire leaders are also likely to exist in toxic work cultures fueled by hyper-aggression and hyper-competition (Mackey et al., 2017). Though there is no excuse for anyone to be a vampire leader, employees whose performance is mediocre or worse are more likely to suffer from abusive supervision than employees who are high performers (Liang et al., 2016; Mackey et al., 2017).

Employees adopt various coping strategies in response to abusive supervision. Whitman and colleagues (2014) found that some employees avoided receiving feedback from abusive leaders to minimize interaction time.

Unfortunately, this increased their burnout as they expended more cognitive resources to plan their work and movements and decreased their access to constructive feedback. Some employees seek refuge with their colleagues which helped them manage the stress and resulted in greater team bonding (Fischer et al., 2021; Tepper, 2000). Conversely, some employees might engage in counterproductive behaviors such as theft, sabotage, or deliberately poor performance as a form of retaliation against their vampire leader (Fischer et al., 2021; Mackey et al., 2017; Tepper, 2000). Even worse, a study found that abused subordinates also engaged in displaced aggression against their family members resulting in increased familial conflict, stress, and relationship strain at home (Carlson et al., 2011). In contrast, one study found that subordinates blamed themselves as opposed to their vampire leaders for the abusive supervision, and increased their sales performance in an effort to thwart the abuse elucidating one context in which abusive supervision actually increased job performance (Ali et al., 2023). Taken together, the research shows that vampire leaders do not simply negatively affect workplace and health-related outcomes for their subordinates but can cultivate a host of negative outcomes for their coworkers, families, and organizations.

Sunlight and garlic will not work on abusive leaders, so what will? The organizational behavior literature offers some guidance. As Whitman and colleagues (2014) found that sustained avoidance of abusive leaders backfires, employees should instead meet to talk to their supervisor about their feelings. In an email, they might request a meeting to let the supervisor know that they would like to talk about ways to improve their working relationship. In the meeting, the employee should start off with curiosity asking the supervisor how they perceive their work relationship? If the supervisor paints a strained picture, then the subordinate can agree they were feeling similarly and ask what they can do to improve their working relationship and what does the supervisor think are the reasons for the strained relationship. If the supervisor paints a rosy picture, then the subordinate can respond with,

> I am happy you want a positive relationship with me because I want one from you too, but honestly, I do not feel like it is at this point. For example, I felt humiliated when you yelled at me during the presentation. Also, you cut me off several times when I was speaking in last week's meeting. I'm sure it might not have been your intention, but those behaviors make me feel unsupported. Were you aware of any of this?

It is natural for people to feel some level of defensiveness when they are receiving critical feedback. As such, subordinates should pay close attention to manage their tone and body language effectively, assume positive intent, be concise with their language, and speak from a place of curiosity as opposed to prosecution. After the supervisor and subordinate agree on some behavioral changes, the subordinate might ask up front to schedule a meeting in two weeks to check-in on their progress. This prescheduled meeting should signal to the leader that the subordinate expects quick behavioral changes.

Subordinates should determine if there are any changes they can make to eliminate any of the abusive supervision. For example, are there real performance decrements that can be improved, does the employee arrive late, does the employee engage in gossip or other undermining behaviors in the workplace, or does the employee embarrass the leader in any ways? Again, no one deserves abusive supervision, but it is prudent that subordinates change the things that are within their power that might improve their current situation.

Finally, subordinates should seek support and guidance from trusted mentors and coworkers. These colleagues can give them a broader perspective and provide much needed emotional support and advice, particularly if they know the abusive leader. If appropriate, they might also intervene on the subordinate's behalf to get any information that might help the subordinate understand what is at the root of the abusive supervision or convince the abusive leader to change their behaviors toward the subordinate. If the above actions do not work, subordinates might also file formal complaints against their abusive supervisor and go through the grievance process. If the grievance process is unsatisfactory or the subordinate is concerned about retaliation, the subordinate should seek a transfer or promotion to another department or resign and seek employment elsewhere. If we are lucky, we will never work for a vampire leader. However, some employees are not so lucky. As such, these strategies might be used to effectively neutralize the vampire.

Reflections in the Mirror

1. What specific organizational and individual factors contribute to the emergence of "vampire leaders," and how can institutions proactively address these factors to prevent abusive supervision?
2. How do the coping strategies employed by employees in response to abusive supervision reflect their broader psychological and social needs, and what role can support systems play in improving these coping mechanisms?
3. In what ways can leaders cultivate a work environment that fosters transparency, respect, and constructive feedback to counteract the negative effects of abusive supervision, and how can these practices be integrated into leadership training programs?

PART II

ONCE BITTEN: TALES OF INTERACTION WITH VAMPIRE LEADERS

INTERLUDE

The 1985 film *Once Bitten* featured a young Jim Carrey as Mark Kendall, a high schooler targeted by a centuries-old vampire, played by Lauren Hutton. This campy horror-comedy became a cult classic as Carrey's star rose. In the spirit of *Once Bitten*, where even the unsuspecting can find themselves caught in the dark dance of the night's creatures, the pages ahead invite you into shadowed chronicles. Just as Mark faced the pull of temptation, you too will explore a world where the night's revelations may feel eerily familiar.

The tales herein, though wrapped in the mystique of obscurity, are anchored in the real-life experiences of those who have crossed paths with the vampires who work among us. To protect the sanctity of these truths—and the safety of those brave enough to share their stories—every name, institution, and landmark has been carefully veiled. This anonymity isn't meant to obscure the truth but rather to shield those who've exposed themselves to the darkness from further harm.

As you delve deeper, keep in mind. Though the details are masked, the essence remains unaltered—a spotlight on the malevolence lurking within certain leadership circles in higher education, and a tribute to the resilience of those who have emerged from the shadows to share their tale.

CHAPTER 6

WHEN VAMPIRE LEADERS CAST LONG SHADOWS

Lenford Sutton
Illinois State University, USA

An important lesson I've learned while in leadership revolves around the concept of "fit" between a leader and an institution. I use the word "fit," but others may use "institutional alignment". If we borrow a similar sentiment from the Christian Bible, the phrase "equally yoked" springs to mind. While much attention is given to a leader's suitability for an organization, the true essence of "fit" lies in the complexities of human relationships, shaped by convergences or divergences in values, expectations, and boundaries. This dynamic is reminiscent of the themes explored in Tomas Alfredson's film *Let the Right One In*, which follows Oskar, a young protagonist, and Eli, a vampire girl.

In their first encounter, Oskar walks through a dark apartment courtyard at night, the shadows cast by surrounding buildings creating an uneasy atmosphere, heightening the tension and sense of foreboding. From the darkness, Eli silently emerges. As they exchange hesitant greetings, the shadows seem to dance around them, emphasizing the secrecy and hidden dangers lurking in the dark.

Much like Eli, some leaders operate in these shadows, avoiding the sunlight of transparency and thriving in secrecy. These "vampire leaders," akin to their mythical counterparts, prefer to operate behind closed doors, concealing their actions and decisions from those they lead. One such instance is exemplified by a provost who failed to reveal the rationale behind critical decisions, such as the allocation of resources for faculty positions.

Vampire Leaders Suck, pages 39–44
Copyright © 2025 by Emerald Publishing Limited
All rights of reproduction in any form reserved.
doi:10.1108/978-1-83708-862-120251006

The role of a department chair is undoubtedly one of the most challenging leadership roles in higher education. When faculty members assume this role, they are tasked with guiding their colleagues through policy changes, curriculum matters, and, most recently, the large-scale disruptions imposed by the Global Pandemic of 2020. Leading such efforts is challenging enough in a shared governance environment, and the ambiguity is further amplified by the duality of serving as both a faculty member and an administrator, nurturing relationships that provide a permission structure to inspire collaboration in a value-driven, highly decentralized learning community.

Small challenges can morph into large-scale problems when there is a lack of clarity in the alignment of values from the top administration to department chairs. This case study describes incidents in which a department chair and faculty believed they were on a clear path to realizing the institution's mission, "To provide a diverse community of students with diverse leadership opportunities" in service to the public good, only to experience an iterative process that darkened what appeared to be a clear pathway to achieving that mission.

Many colleagues who shy away from assuming department chair roles regard the position as a proverbial crash dummy in the collision of values and perspectives that occupy the higher education enterprise (Chan & Evans, 2023). It can be quite perilous for department chairs tasked with developing relationships with colleagues, the Dean, and the President's Teams, as any imbalance in these relationships may be easily misconstrued as an allegiance to one side over the other (Hecht et al., 1999).

One of the most frustrating events I've experienced occurred after my faculty colleagues and I collaborated to establish new relationships with non-traditional graduate students from underserved communities, expanding our enrollment by 54% in 2 years. From my perspective, there was a high level of cohesion and agreement about our values and establishing these new relationships with students aligned with the college and university's mission, which were one and the same. Faculty routinely practiced telling stories of how our collective work enunciated the institutional ethos.

However, the true nature of vampire leadership began to reveal itself, casting long shadows over our efforts. Despite the apparent alignment with the institution's mission and the success of our initiatives, there was a disconnect between the values and expectations at the top and those of the department. This disconnect, fueled by a lack of transparency and open communication, created an environment where the department chair and faculty felt they were operating in the dark, much like Oskar navigating the shadows of the courtyard.

Vampire leaders thrive in such environments, wielding their power through secrecy and obfuscation, leaving those they lead to navigate the unknown and question the true motives behind decisions. It is in these shadows that the true danger of vampire leadership lies, as it erodes trust, stifles collaboration, and undermines the very mission and values that should be at the core of an institution.

In such situations, it becomes imperative for principled leaders to shed light on the shadows cast by vampire leaders, exposing their actions to the purifying light of transparency and accountability. Only then can an institution truly thrive, fostering an atmosphere of trust, collaboration, and shared purpose—a stark contrast to the nightmarish realm of vampire leaders and their shadowy machinations. While this chapter primarily examines failed leadership, it is crucial to highlight the individuals affected by discussing who is at stake here (pun not intended).

Alexis Washington, a high school English teacher and a single mother of five boys was enrolled in a doctoral program in education management at a non-profit institution. Alexis decided that she needed to expand her career opportunities and a better standard of living for her boys by pursuing a doctoral degree in leadership that may lead to obtaining a leadership position and increased compensation. When I met Alexis, age 37, at one of our college information sessions and social gatherings, she shared that she had taken 2 years of courses online with the institution, spending at least 20 hours a week on homework assignments. However, when she completed the coursework, she needed help getting direction or mentoring from the faculty that would allow her to write her dissertation. She scheduled seven appointments with an advisor or faculty member over two semesters, and each meeting was canceled within 24 hours of its start.

At the same time, her two oldest boys, 12 and 13, had moved from elementary to junior high school and struggled to adjust from having one to two teachers to six to eight in their new school setting. Their historically strong grades declined, and they often found themselves out of class on a disciplinary referral to the Assistant Principal's office. Alexis believed that if she could complete her doctoral studies, she would have a better chance of leading a school learning community and improving the educational experiences for her children. Alexis explained that she had accumulated $124,000 in student loan debt for the 64 hours of graduate tuition and was frustrated by the lack of support for her research efforts. We asked her if she had decided on a dissertation topic and the related literature, and she politely asked what a dissertation is. "Oh, you mean my prospectus?" Lastly, Alexis explained that she and eight of her teacher colleagues started the program simultaneously, and they still need to complete their research and graduate.

When the associate chair and I told Alexis's story to our department colleagues, a few said they had heard of other teachers in other schools who had similar circumstances after enrolling in a for-profit college, which offered more convenience but certainly more expensive. The associate chair suggested that we assemble an ad hoc committee to consider ways to help working adult students like Alexis. After much debate about the quality and image of our graduate programming, the department faculty, in a 20–2 vote, agreed to petition the graduate school and ask for a 2-year waiver of the 40% limit on coursework that can be transferred from other accredited institutions and used to satisfy graduation requirements. Our colleagues agreed to name this empathy-driven innovation "Operation Rescue with Quality." The waiver was granted, and the ceiling on the percent of transferable coursework was raised to 85%.

In 2018, Alexis and two colleagues graduated with a Doctor of Education during the fall semester. It was a very proud moment to watch Alexis's sons witness the completion of her educational journey. Since then, she has served as an assistant principal in an elementary school and is now the principal of a STEM junior high school, serving 1,200 students with 89 faculty and staff. Alexis is also a fierce advocate of our programs and an officer in the alumni association. Since then, seventeen other adult learners have completed their graduate studies through "Operation Rescue with Quality."

That same year 2018, five departmental faculty colleagues retired or left the university altogether. In response, the department leadership requested the opportunity to search for five tenure-track colleagues to replenish faculty ranks, only to be denied any additional faculty searches for three years. The next sequence of events underscores the heart of a secretive, vampire leader who uses her charm to show favor to "her people" while ignoring those whose value she has no use. Those who afford her the "blood" she needs are provided favor.

When colleagues pressed for why no searches were granted, no clear explanation was given. Ultimately, the provost failed or chose not to respond. However, a committee of colleagues analyzed the enrollment-faculty conditions of similarly situated departments and discovered that even departments with challenging enrollments were provided the opportunity to search for new colleagues. Notability, the department that was afforded the opportunity to hire faculty, despite declining enrollment, shared the discipline with the provost, who emerged from their ranks. Even more, the provost was overtly friendly and cordial with this group during whole faculty meetings. She was often seen laughing with them, complete with pats on the back and hand claps of joviality. In contrast, toward the higher education administration department and most other departments, she was described as cold and distant.

"She is dark and lifeless," one of the faculty members said.

"Dark and lifeless" are common descriptors for a vampire. Likewise, as she showed overt favor to one group and seeming disdain to another, the provost exemplified shapeshifting, also like a vampire.

In 2019 a new dean arrived, and the higher education administration department faculty were told there needed to be a "data-driven method" to award additional faculty. To us, it sounded like a load of inorganic cow manure. What were we thinking to believe that increasing enrollment would be followed by efforts to secure the necessary faculty to serve a growing department? We were wrong, but we stayed true to the mission with the resources we had until; eventually, overworked colleagues began to feel disrespected and underappreciated, prompting a retreat from our values, decreasing engagement, less caring, less sharing, foregone innovation, and common cause for our work. Like Oscar and Eli's first meeting, an uncomfortable atmosphere ensued among the faculty, "heightening the tension and sense of foreboding."

As the department chair engaged with upper administration to secure the alignment of goals and values, he soon sensed what Picca and Feagan (2007) termed "front-stage and back-state activity" underpinning the radical attitudes and behaviors exhibited by persons in private settings. Argyris and Schon have described similar moments in which a leader may have an aspirational interest in an organizational phenomenon but is reluctant to implement the same in practical ways (Argyris & Schön, 1974). If we look to Van Wart et al. (2021) for explanation, this behavior could be characterized by bloodsucking, leader's self-serving, manipulative practices come at the price of the institution's mission, values, and stakeholders.

The nomenclature in this scenario is less important than the darkness and blindness the academic unit functioned in. In this case, several root causes can be identified, including the lack of a coherent policy and procedure to secure tenure line searches. However, even in the absence of clear policies, effective, sacrificial leaders who lean into transparency, do not operate in secrecy. In this situation, affirmation of searches seemed to be grounded in the leader's personal affinity for various units on campus. Therefore, the department found it difficult to successfully request the additional resources needed for the unit to function and serve students.

When senior faculty wrote a letter to the provost requesting an opportunity to meet and discuss needed resources, they became frustrated after eight weeks and having not received a response. So, a small group penned a letter to the President of the University requesting a meeting, something that did not sit well with the provost.

It's undeniable that conditions deteriorated rapidly from that juncture onward, especially as faculty felt as though they remained in the dark about how resources are allocated within an academic unit. For these stakeholders, this provost was not the "right one". In the realm of higher education leadership, where inspiration serves as the primary catalyst for achieving goals, objectives, and student outcomes, there are certainly more favorable outcomes to aspire to. Despite the crisis and misunderstandings that ensued, it is essential to remember the guiding light of your organizational values, even when operating under the shadow of covert leadership. As in Alfredson's film *Let the Right One In*, where darkness and secrecy pervade, it's crucial to rely on your principles to navigate through challenging times.

Dark Reflections and Nightfall Scenarios

1. Reflect on the concept of "institutional alignment" or "fit" between a leader and an institution. How have you observed or experienced the impact of misalignment between leadership values and institutional goals? What strategies can be employed to ensure that leaders and institutions remain aligned, fostering a culture of transparency and shared purpose?
2. Scenario: As a department chair, you have noticed that the new provost exhibits favoritism toward certain departments, granting them resources and support while neglecting others, including yours. This has created an environment of frustration and low morale among your faculty.
    - How would you approach the provost to discuss the perceived favoritism and advocate for equitable resource allocation without jeopardizing your department's standing?
    - What steps can you take within your department to maintain morale and productivity despite the lack of support from the provost?
3. Scenario: A colleague has come to you feeling demoralized and unsupported due to the provost's secretive and manipulative leadership style. They are considering leaving the institution due to the toxic environment.
    - How would you counsel your colleague and provide support to help them navigate this challenging situation?
    - What initiatives can you implement to foster a more supportive and transparent departmental culture, mitigating the negative impact of the provost's leadership on your team?

CHAPTER 7

TRIUMVIRATE OF DARKNESS: CHRONICLES OF VAMPIRE LEADERS IN THE ACADEMY

Kevin A. Rolle
Alabama State University, USA

After more than three decades in higher education, one is bound to accumulate a treasure trove of experiences—some enlightening, others downright sinister. My journey through higher education administration, which was enriched further by a transformative stint as an American Council on Education fellow, has been no exception. This immersive experience allowed me to traverse the breadth of our educational system, from Ivy League institutions to the bustling campuses of international counterparts. Along the way, I've witnessed a spectrum of leadership behaviors and administrative structures, each leaving an indelible mark on my perspective.

In hindsight, I'd like to believe that my experiences have been formed through wisdom and insight and that I was guided toward fostering positive outcomes for our institutions and their stakeholders. I'd also like to believe that the same is true for all who I've shared space. Alas, reality has a way of punctuating our illusions, for I've encountered my fair share of folly and darkness in the annals of academia.

The stories I'm about to share are not my own. I count myself fortunate to have been spared the clutches of leaders who could rival the most nefarious of vampires. Yet, as I reflect upon past encounters, I cannot help but acknowledge the insidious nature of certain leadership behaviors.

Vampire Leaders Suck, pages 45–51
Copyright © 2025 by Emerald Publishing Limited
All rights of reproduction in any form reserved.
doi:10.1108/978-1-83708-862-120251007

In my earlier years, before the wisdom of silver streaks and the humility of experience settled upon me, I might have dismissed these behaviors as mere quirks of personality or differences in leadership style. However, thanks to the illuminating insights of Van Wart et al. (2021) and the diligent efforts of Patrice W. Glenn Jones, the academy's new Van Helsing, I've come to recognize them for what they truly are—manifestations of "vampire leadership."

Now, let me assure you, I do not believe myself to have ever exhibited such vampiric tendencies. My compass has always pointed steadfastly toward the best interests of our students and stakeholders. I recognize my facility as a human, so I accept the reality that others may hold different perception of me. I am humbled by the notion that the experiences I have shared with others may shed light on the shadows cast by dark leaders; thus, I present to you a trilogy of vignettes. These narratives, akin to the cautionary tales of Count Dracula and Count Orlok, serve as stark reminders of the perilous terrain that lurks in academia.

Sarah's Sorrow

Few experiences stand out as vividly as the tale of Sarah, a diligent and passionate member of our team, who unwittingly found herself ensnared in the Machiavellian machinations of a leader whose cunning mirrored that of a vampire. The tension between Sarah and Joel, the vampire leader, was regularly palatable and made others uncomfortable. One particular exchange between Sarah and Joel encapsulates the insidious nature of vampire leaders' wily tactics.

It was during a team meeting where Sarah, brimming with enthusiasm, presented a well-researched proposal aimed at improving student retention rates.

"I believe this initiative could be a game-changer for our institution," she declared, her eyes shining with conviction.

Joel, much like the cunning Count Dracula from Bram Stoker's classic novel, feigned enthusiasm.

"That's fine work, Sarah," he proclaimed, offering a round of applause seem to beam in the eyes of their colleges but was thwarted.

"But," Joel express. "I'm not sure that's the right solution for our institution."

And behind closed doors, the leader adopted a more sinister demeanor, akin to Dracula's transformation from a charming nobleman to a bloodthirsty monster. In a private conversation with Sarah, he subtly undermined her proposal, casting doubt on its feasibility and questioning her competence.

"While your intentions are admirable, I fear this plan may be overly ambitious," he said, his words dripping with condescension. "Are you certain you have the necessary experience to spearhead such an endeavor?"

Sarah, taken aback by the sudden shift in tone, defended her ideas with facts and data. "But the research clearly shows that this approach has been successful at other institutions. I'm confident it can work here as well."

Joel employed subtle manipulative techniques, gaslighting and veiled threats of repercussion, to dissuade her from pursuing her initiative further.

"I appreciate your enthusiasm, but perhaps you should reconsider," said Joel. "Such an undertaking could be... detrimental to your future prospects here."

Sarah left the conversation feeling disheartened and demoralized, doubting her abilities and questioning whether her contributions were truly valued within the organization.

Little did she know that this was just one of many instances where the vampire leader would use their wily tactics to maintain control and suppress dissent within the team. Much like Count Dracula, who sought to exert dominance over those around him, this leader thrived on the fear and uncertainty they instilled in their subordinates.

However, in a twist of Machiavellian cunning, Joel unveiled a slightly modified version of Sarah's proposal, presenting it as his own brainchild during a meeting with the board of trustees.

"I've been giving this issue a great deal of thought," he proclaimed, "and I believe I have a solution that could revolutionize our approach to student retention."

As I sat in that meeting, witnessing the vampire leader take ownership of Sarah's idea, I couldn't help but feel a sense of outrage at the brazen display of Machiavellian behavior. This leader's actions were a calculated move to consolidate power and undermine any potential threats to their authority, even if it meant appropriating the ideas of others and crushing their spirits in the process.

As I reflect on Sarah's experience, it serves as a sobering reminder of the dangers of allowing such Machiavellian behavior to go unchecked within our institutions. It underscores the importance of fostering a culture of transparency, accountability, and mutual respect, where individuals like Sarah feel empowered to voice their ideas without fear of reprisal or manipulation.

Nightshade and Moonlight

The second narrative I must share presents a stark warning of a leader who wielded power like a skilled illusionist, manipulating those around her with the finesse of a master puppeteer. This leader, known to us as Dr. Nightshade, possessed a remarkable ability to adapt her demeanor to suit any situation. Her charm was intoxicating, drawing unsuspecting souls into her orbit with ease. Yet beneath her charismatic facade lurked a darker agenda, one fueled by ambition and a thirst for control.

One fateful day, rumors of Dr. Nightshade's Machiavellian tactics reached my ears, painting a disturbing picture of manipulation and deceit. It appeared that Dr. Nightshade had taken a keen interest in a rising star within our midst—Professor Moonlight, a bright and promising faculty member with aspirations of and influence toward assuming a leadership role at the institution. It was clear to many that Moonlight posed a potential threat to Nightshade's own position, and so she set her sights on him with a predatory gleam in her eye.

At first, Moonlight was enchanted by Dr. Nightshade's allure. Her apparent generosity seemed to promise great opportunities for advancement. She kept him close, assigning him to participate on committees that she led. Yet as time passed, the true nature of Nightshade's intentions began to reveal itself. She employed subtle manipulations, whispered words of flattery mixed with oblique threats, all designed to bend Moonlight to her will.

Vampire leaders frequently alter their personas to garner support and loyalty from those they favor. However, over time, those who are favored may unwittingly become victims of the vampire leader's insatiable appetite for control and power. They transform from under their favor to becoming their flavor. Through a combination of charisma and manipulation, individuals who align themselves with the vampire leader risk losing their own sense of identity and purpose, succumbing to the leader's influence. They are metaphorically bitten and transformed, much like the behavior of Count Orlok in the silent film *Nosferatu*.

In just this way, Moonlight found himself ensnared in Nightshade's web of deceit before long. He was no longer the independent thinker and aspiring leader he once was; instead, he had become a mere pawn in Nightshade's quest for dominance. Like a vampire creating other vampires, Nightshade had drained Moonlight of his autonomy and integrity, leaving him a mere shadow of his former self.

But the story does not end there, my friends. No, for Nightshade's thirst for power was insatiable. She continued to shape-shift and manipulate, ascending the ranks of our institution with alarming speed. Along the way, she left a trail of shattered dreams and fractured trust in her wake, her influence spreading like a dark cloud over our once harmonious community.

Devon's Rule

At a former institution where I served, there existed a figure of considerable influence, a vampire leader we will call Devon Rule. Devon exuded an aura of entitlement and superiority that left no room for doubt about his self-perceived status. He moved through the campus with an air of smugness, his demeanor practically daring others to challenge his authority.

Conversations with Devon were often one-sided, his discourse revolving around his own accomplishments and supposed superiority. "That's 'Dr. Rule' to you," he'd curtly correct anyone who dared address him informally. "I'm here as the epitome of academic excellence, with years of experience to guide this institution to greatness," he'd proclaim, his arrogance evident in every word. "Those who can't keep up can find the door."

Under Devon's reign, faculty and staff felt like mere instruments in his grand scheme for domination. His leadership style leaned more toward dictatorship than guidance, and he made no effort to hide his belief in his own infallibility. He saw the stakeholders of the institution as expendable assets, with little regard for their individual aspirations or well-being.

"I am the mastermind behind this institution's success," Devon would declare, his voice dripping with self-satisfaction. "Without me, it would crumble into oblivion, lost in the annals of history."

Any attempt to challenge Devon's authority was swiftly met with retribution, as he crushed dissent with ruthless efficiency. He made it clear that he was the captain of the ship, and anyone who dared oppose him would face the consequences.

In Bram Stoker's "Dracula," there's a scene where the vampire Count Dracula reveals his commanding presence and dominance over his minions. In this particular scene, Dracula stands at the center of his dark and eerie castle, surrounded by his loyal followers who hang on his every word. With his piercing gaze and authoritative voice, Dracula issues commands to his subjects, who obey without question, driven by both fear and reverence for their master.

Dracula's demeanor in this scene is one of absolute confidence and superiority. He exudes an aura of power and control, commanding the attention and obedience of all who stand before him. His words carry weight, and his followers dare not defy him, knowing the consequences of disobedience could be dire.

Similarly, Devon Rule's behavior echoes Dracula's commanding presence. Like Dracula, Devon stood at the center of his domain, surrounded by those who looked to him for guidance and direction. His demeanor was one of unyielding confidence and authority, and he ruled over his domain with an iron fist, demanding unwavering obedience from those under his control. Just as Dracula asserts his dominance over his minions, so too did Devon Rule exert his control over those within his sphere of influence.

Confronting the Vampires Among Us

As I conclude my exploration of the harrowing tales of Joel, Nightshade, and Devon, it becomes evident that the traits of entitlement, superiority, manipulation, and shape-shifting, along with the other characteristics of vampire leadership, pose significant challenges to academic institutions and their communities. In reflecting on these narratives, it strikes a personal chord within me. These vampire-like behaviors not only foster a toxic atmosphere but also sow seeds of fear, distrust, and disengagement among our colleagues and students. The impact is palpable, as morale suffers, and resentment festers among team members who feel undervalued and demoralized. We also lose talent. Moreover, the unpredictability of vampire leaders makes it difficult for us to navigate our professional topography with confidence. Instability reigns, stifling progress and innovation, as dissent is silenced, and alternative viewpoints are suppressed.

Yet, amidst the darkness, there is hope. It is imperative for us, as leaders, to take proactive measures to combat the negative influences of vampire leadership. By fostering a culture of transparency, accountability, and mutual respect, we can begin to heal the wounds inflicted by these toxic behaviors. Leading by example, with humility, integrity, and empathy, we can cultivate a supportive work environment where all stakeholders feel valued and empowered to contribute their ideas and perspectives.

Through education and awareness initiatives, we can empower our colleagues to recognize and address toxic behaviors, ensuring that our institutions remain facilitators of excellence and integrity in higher education. As we navigate the shadows cast by vampire leaders, let us remain steadfast in our commitment to creating a brighter future for our academic communities—one built on collaboration, empowerment, and shared purpose.

Dark Reflections and Nightfall Scenarios

1. Reflect on the ways in which vampire leaders can erode trust and collaboration within academic institutions. How can leaders and members of academic communities recognize and address these toxic behaviors early to prevent long-term damage? What specific actions can be taken to foster a culture of transparency, accountability, and mutual respect?

2. Scenario: You are a department chair at a university and notice that one of your colleagues, Dr. Moonlight, who was once a vibrant and independent thinker, seems to have become a mere extension of Dr. Nightshade, a senior administrator known for her manipulative tactics. Dr. Moonlight's innovative ideas are now being credited to Dr. Nightshade, and his enthusiasm has noticeably waned.
   - How would you approach Dr. Moonlight to discuss your observations and offer support without making him feel defensive or embarrassed?

- What steps can you take to address the broader issue of Dr. Nightshade's toxic leadership within the institution while protecting yourself and your colleagues from potential retaliation?
- How can you promote a healthier work environment in your department to ensure that faculty members feel valued, empowered, and recognized for their contributions?

CHAPTER 8

MANIPULATION AND THE LAIR OF MEDIOCRITY

Roswell Lawrence Jr.
University of Georgia, USA

Suppose you ask the professionals I lead about my leadership style. In that case, each person will likely provide a distinct description that seems different from the depiction of others within the same office and even on the same day. One may say, "He's a great leader. He allows me the space to make my own decisions and offers sound support and direction when I need it." A second team member's response may provide a stark contrast as they explain how I provide plenty of support along with succinct and clear step-by-step instructions. Yet a third may provide what even may sound like a complaint of the same behaviors I give another: "He tends to micromanage my behaviors and restrict me from what I think are simple actions related to my job. He screens what I do." All would be accurate.

I have always been on a path of leadership; I see leadership as a continuous journey of evolution. Even as a young man in my family with older siblings, there was an expectation to lead from those around me, both young and old. I cultivated my natural leadership strengths: galvanizing others, communicating adaptively, springing to action in a crisis, emphasizing professional development, and insistence on personal growth. My leadership style is like a liberal arts education; I, too, hope to be broad, transferable, and flexible. I prefer to lead in ways that allow me to get out of the way and be supportive; however, through mentors and personal and professional development, I can also provide the necessary leadership influence to motivate my team.

I highlight my leadership style to underscore the leadership continuum even as characterized within one individual. In addition to being nimble in leadership and personality, I am resilient. Some may see these adjectives (i.e., nimble and resilient) as antonyms, but they are true, nonetheless. They speak to how I exist in any space and how my way of thinking and leading is rooted in the man I am—one who observes, analyzes, questions, and acts almost simultaneously.

Thus, when confronted with the phrase "vampire leadership," I considered the variability of this toxic misnomer. For me, the word "leadership" should be qualified by favorable outcomes. Leadership and management are certainly used synonymously, but few would argue that these actions in practice are the same. People are often managers by their titles and ability to maintain things as they are, but some never pick up the mantle to lead or evoke growth. Such, too, is the case in the realm of higher education.

In his 1989 book, *On Becoming a Leader*, Warren Bennis, who is often identified as a pioneer in the field of leadership studies, wrote, "The manager accepts the status quo; the leader changes it" (p. 39). This quote is at the center of this narrative. However, for the sake of this volume, I will lean into the language "vampire leadership" in solidarity with my academic counterparts. However, I find it necessary to make a distinction between "manager" and "leader" for the purpose of the narrative that I will share.

The qualities of vampire leader that strike the strongest accord with my experiences is the quality of shapeshifting as described by Van Wart et al. (2021). However, it does not truly capture the full scope of the experience I will share. Again, I cannot reiterate how those who share these qualities are not leaders; they are managers.

Extending beyond the capacity to shift in shape, a vampire manager thrives on his inherent privilege and uses it to maintain his position of power. Much like vampires, they feed off the opportunities and resources available without putting in the necessary effort or demonstrating actual competence. Instead of using their position to uplift others and drive positive change, they rely on manipulation and exploitation to further their own agenda, leaving a trail of disenchantment and stifled growth in his wake. Herein, this vampire manager will be known as Edward.

Something else you should know about me is that I have never entered a race without the true desire to win. Even if I were lined up in the starting blocks with Usain Bolt as my competitor, I would run the race to win. It goes without saying that I probably could not beat Bolt in a foot race, but that is beside the point. I certainly would train, stretch, take my mark, listen intently for the start and run to the best of my ability.

As a mid-level higher education leader with "manager" in my title, I was excited when finally allowed, after weeks of intensely debating my desire and need for professional development, to attend a national convening that pulled both higher education and industry organizations together to share efficient practices, celebrate praiseworthy accomplishments, and promote future promise. After returning from the conference, the organizers invited me to present at the next conveying.

My supervisor, Edward, held the most senior position in our office. For some people, Edward's towering frame, piercing blue eyes, and resounding baritone voice could cover them in intimidation like that of a settling fog on a mountain drive. For me, he did not have this effect. Even as a young Roswell Lawrence, Jr, I was raised to be a man who upholds the name I share with my father. This means to think for yourself and stand ten toes down as you speak your truth. While I was not intimidated by Edward, it would not be true if I said that Edward did not affect me.

Upon sharing with him that I was extended an invitation to present at our national conference, Edward's resistance first appeared in a common form among those who aim to manipulate.

"Your role normally doesn't attend the national session," he said.

Telling me what happens typically and how what I am requesting has never proved an effective approach, so I persisted by spending days preparing a presentation to convey the value in my attendance, a series of measures and returns on investments that only seemed to amplify Edward's opposing persistence in disagreement. I was frustrated.

Sitting in my office one day, Edward emerged at the door almost as if his 6'4" frame defied the laws of gravity and hovered in through the nearly visible barrier of frustration that occupied the air in my office. He closed the door behind him, positioned his butt on the edge of the seat opposite my desk; he leaned his torso back to the backrest of the chair, leaving a vacuum of air behind himself. He sulked his body further in the chair and stretched his long legs beyond the unseen perimeter that existed beyond my desk into my space. He was in a far too comfortable a posture for the conversation that followed:

"Roswell," he began. "There's no reason for you to attend the conference."

"This is a great opportunity, Edward," I retorted. "We have the opportunity to be a top unit in the state and certainly number one in the region if we . . ."

Before I could even finish my sentence, it was as though I had provided Edward with the language and cause to project his standard of privileged mediocrity on me.

"We don't want to be number one, Roswell," Edward declared as if his statement provided an unprotest-able fiat of professional existence. "When you're number one, there's a lot of attention on you. And we don't need that. Heck, we don't even want to be in the top five. We want to just want to fly under the radar."

The physical performance accompanying his final sentence accelerated its delivery. Positioning his hand horizontally near his face as if it were a humanized airplane, he waved his flying hand through the air. Even though I knew he could be shortsighted and lackadaisical, his mentality still astonished me.

Disbelief fell upon my face, and I felt depleted. When faced with those whose privilege allows them to enter a race *not* to win, my mind is often transported to the Jim Crow era in the southern United States, a time when systematic and strategic efforts were taken to reduce African American excellence and to promote mediocrity to debilitate a race of people and stifle achievement. The irony was not lost on me: an African American man in a standoff with a European descendant seemingly not motivated by racial bias but by a pervasive institutional mediocrity. This is not to say that I believe Edward's motives were motivated by racism. It is just a fact worth noting.

What I know for certain is that Edward's privilege allowed him to not only remain ineffective but also fertilize the same quality of feebleness and lackluster middling for those he managed. This is a privilege I do not have, nor is it a liberty I would take if I could.

Edward also used jocund discourse and maneuvers to hide the limits of his knowledge and capacity. He sought to make others laugh, another common deflection scheme. And if his own words are not enough, evidence of Edward's comfort with mediocracy is reflected in the fact roughly 20 years after completing his course work in a doctoral degree program, Edward remains "all but dissertation" even though all other directors hold terminal degrees which remains an expectation for the role.

Edward's vampire-like, shapeshifting quality did not stop with his attempt to overtly plant seeds of "flying under the radar" among his stakeholders and waiting with stagnation for a barren harvest to yield. He also leveraged the resources at his disposal—namely money—to control and misuse team members for his own ends. Whenever he wanted a team member to take on tasks that simplified his own job, he would suggest adding a financial stipend to their salary. However, he would also threaten to withdraw this stipend if things didn't proceed as he envisioned. I've seen Edward use this manipulative maneuver repeatedly, even when a team member disagreed. It was not only unethical but also a drain on the institution's resources and deeply damaging to the morale of those under his influence.

When I look to vampire fiction to identify the parallel of this behavior, I am reminded of the relationship dynamics of the main characters in *Interview with a Vampire*. In the film, the vampire Lestat uses manipulation to control his protégé, Louis, and the young vampire Claudia. Lestat offers knowledge and promises of eternal life to entice Louis to stay with him despite Louis' moral objections to their vampire lifestyle. Similarly, Lestat manipulates Claudia by turning her into a vampire at a young age, ensuring her dependence on him for survival and knowledge about their kind.

Lestat's manipulation involves offering and withholding his approval and knowledge, akin to the way Charlie used financial incentives to control team members. Both examples show a powerful figure exploiting his authority and the vulnerabilities of others to meet personal objectives, often at a significant emotional and ethical cost to those being manipulated.

I enjoyed my job, and even as a manager in title, I conducted myself as a leader in practice—a leader who values differences, possesses interpersonal savvy, builds informal relationships and networks, collaborates well, and cultivates effective teams. At least these are my strengths, according to my Korn Ferry 360 assessment, and I agree with them. No leader can call him or herself by such a label if cultivating excellence and promoting individualized and collective development are not driving pillars for approaching leadership. Indeed, not everyone has to think they have a shot at beating Bolt in a race, but each leader should at least get in the starting blocks and run as fast as possible.

As someone committed to fostering excellence and promoting development, I found Edward's vision impossible to support. Yet, strangely, many did. The office under his watch was often a stagnant pool—devoid of life, motivation, progress, or growth. Shortly after that conversation in my office, I resigned and moved on to a role where my leadership could flourish and would make a difference.

One of the most detrimental outcomes of vampirism, as my colleagues would agree, is the loss of talent. Vampires in the academy bleed their constituents of their desire, capacity, and energy, and for those who are driven to advance institutional missions and impact student learning, such environments feel like coffins. Edward was a true "bloodsucker, dream crusher bleeding me dry" reminiscent of the manipulative figures in vampire lore and in Olivia Rodrigo's aptly titled song, *Vampire*.

In the end, I chose to seek an environment where leadership means challenging the status quo as well as uplifting others, not holding them back. Writing about this experience is a stark reminder of the responsibility leaders must not only enhance the organization but to respect, guide, and nurture team members. True leaders are always being led as they continue to learn and are mentored by other leaders to lead more completely.

Dark Reflections and Nightfall Scenarios

1. Reflect on the differences between leadership and management as discussed in the chapter. How can recognizing these differences help educational leaders avoid the pitfalls of "vampire management"? What steps can you take to ensure you are fostering growth and excellence rather than maintaining the status quo?
2. Consider the concept of "shapeshifting" in leadership. Have you encountered leaders who manipulate their personas to maintain power and control? How did their behavior impact the

morale and productivity of their team? What strategies can be implemented to recognize and counteract such manipulation in academic settings?

3. Scenario: You are a mid-level higher education leader who recently observed your supervisor, Edward, using financial incentives to manipulate team members into taking on tasks that primarily benefit him. You have also noticed that this behavior is causing frustration and low morale among your colleagues.

- How would you address the issue with Edward, considering the power dynamics and potential repercussions for your career?
- What steps can you take to support your colleagues and foster a more positive and collaborative work environment despite Edward's manipulative tactics?
- How can you leverage your role to promote transparency, accountability, and ethical behavior within your team and the broader institution?

CHAPTER 9

EMERGING FROM THE SNAKE PIT

Patrice W. Glenn Jones
Alabama State University, USA

The narratives in previous chapters underscored many of the same characteristics outlined by the seminal article by Van Wart et al. (2021). However, a characteristic that was not previously discussed, yet prevails as vital for vampire leaders to thrive, is the existence of a master vampire who possesses greater authority than the vampire leader. In some cases, this master vampire proves a bigger threat and affords vampire leaders the space and perhaps even the permission to sink their fangs into an institution.

I am not a fan of snakes. And like vampires, snakes are known for their fangs. For years, I have familiarized myself with American's greatest fears, and each time I do, snakes appear somewhere on the top of that list. Obviously, the fear is associated with the venom that has the potential to cause fatality. While all snakes are not lethal or even venomous, those that are in their species make it difficult for the rest. A few years ago when a six-foot-long rattlesnake basked in the sun on my front yard, I was truly grateful for the built in alert system that is the creatures rattle adorned tail. As I carried grocery bags through my front door, the rattlesnake alerted me that we were in the same space—a space I was all too willing to yield to the snake. On that day, I appreciated that creatures' rattles, for I was alerted to what I was dealing with.

The story I've chosen to share highlights such a senior leader who not only validated the behavior of a vampire leader but justified and defended this behavior. Unlike the rattlesnake in my yard, I was not alerted to the leader's threat. The bulk of the narrative shares the behavior of the vampire leader, but through the subtext, you will understand why the senior leader's actions are emphasized.

Slithering through the institution with fang-like malice, this senior leader enabled the vampire's transgressions. Could this leader himself move like a vampire or even a crony doing the vampire leader's venomous bidding? Many people misassume that those who sit at the zenith of leadership or hold the "top" title are those who wield the power. Such is not always the case. The dynamics of power can play out through what we know about each other, do for each other, or hold over each other.

The leader at the zenith of position, in this narrative, did not seem to hold the power. Or maybe he did? But, with every forked tongue defense of the vampire's action, it became clearer that the senior leader had embraced the role of master vampire, granting permission for the bloodsucking subordinate to spread her serpentine influence across the campus and beyond.

The Story

When I joined Twister College (an obvious pseudonym), it didn't take long to recognize the resident vampire leader. She stood in the spotlight despite her poor reputation and ill received disposition. Few truly respected her, and many seemed disinterested in her leadership, turned off by her existence, and disdained by her discourse. However, many were unwilling to express their dissatisfaction, a quiet resistance resulting from her relationship with the college president.

"I'm not sure why," one would say, "but she has his ear."

Dr. Adder, a fitting pseudonym for our purposes, presented herself as the chair of my hiring committee. When I was offered a position as an administrator in the Office of Academic Affairs, I inquired about the possibility of also having a faculty appointment.

"We don't do that here," she hissed.

Later, I discovered that Twister did, in fact, "do that." She simply chose not to extend the offer, likely because she lacked the instructional experience necessary for her own faculty appointment. Indeed, vampire leaders suck, and they don't want you to have what they do not.

A series of negative exchanges ensued early in my time at Twister. When I took the initiative to communicate with an external organization to learn more about them, I received a curt and poorly written email from Adder, who was the college's liaison with the organization. She directed me not to contact the organization, as that was her responsibility. On another occasion, I received a scathing email from her after inadvertently excluding her from a group message. Although she was not my direct supervisor, she took it upon herself to exert her authority over me and to communicate, with clarity, that I was her subordinate. Some people just need to feel powerful.

During group discussions, I would casually mention working on research or writing an article, and she would shamelessly respond, "I want to be added to that." Never a request to collaborate on solutions but a demand to leech off my efforts. A fundamental characteristic of a vampire leader.

As a culminating experience for me, so I thought, she made a mockery of herself with Take Flight Association (pseudonym for a national association) during a Zoom conversation that left me wanting to slide under the damn table from sheer embarrassment. We were discussing ways Twister's team could secure funding to match those that Take Flight Association would secure. At the suggestion of working to secure funds through notices of funding, this vampire leader responded both incongruously and inanely.

"Oh, I gets grants," she said, sounding stupid as hell. "You are speaking to the person who got the largest grant in Twister College history."

Now, I cannot make this up; she used those words. The English composition teacher in me cringed as I typed those actual words, and as much as I wish these were fabrications or sensationalized writings, her comments are true. And to think, this was just one of the several "special projects" that the college president handed to her. I must emphasize; while the details surrounding this story are presented with anonymity, the discourse is nearly an exact replica of what this "leader" said, including the bad grammar, "I gets grants," which is a direct quote.

I later discovered that the grant "gotten" was another situation where Adder asked to be added to a proposal she didn't contribute to. The skilled team of researchers obliged, and now she was taking credit for acquiring the funds in the most illogical context.

Adder's relentless pursuit of opportunities such as grant applications, research, and publications mirrors the insatiable thirst of a vampire for blood. However, instead of seeking sustenance, this vampire leader seeks to enhance her own stature within the academic community. Just as traditional vampires crave blood to maintain their strength and vitality, Adder craves recognition and accomplishments to bolster her position as a respected academic.

The parallels of dealing with a vampire-like snake prompted me to remember one of the most famous scenes from Quentin Tarantino's *From Dusk Till Dawn*. The scene starts with a bartender inside the Titty Twister (i.e., the name of the bar) announcing the next act: "The epitome of evil, the most sinister woman to ever dance on the face of this earth. Bow your head. Kneel and worship at the feet of Santanico Pandemonium!" It went something like that.

Then, Salma Hayek, portraying Santanico, appears wearing a giant feather headdress and cape like an ancient goddess. She opens the cape to reveal a tiny bikini. She closes the cape. When she opens her cape again, we see a large albino python wrapped around her nearly-naked body, as if it appeared there magically. Santanico writhes around on stage with the snake, accompanied by some sultry guitar rock music, until her nearly naked assistants remove the python, and she walks downstairs and onto a tabletop.

Upon seeing blood, she gets a crazed look in her eyes, turns into a snake-woman vampire, and attacks one of the male characters. While her body doesn't fully transform into a scaled reptile, her head does, complete with a few reptilian markings on her body. After all, she is "the epitome of evil," a true snake.

Much like Santanico, Adder's behavior was alarming and damn-near unbelievable. Despite a litany of unethical behavior, including copying and pasting accreditation documents and complaints of harassment and workplace toxicity, she was consistently promoted, and her poison continued to spread. One day, I received a phone call that put the "nail in the coffin" for me.

"Patrice, she is a snake," the voice exclaimed.

"Hey," I replied to the familiar voice. "Who? Who are you talking about?"

"Adder!" she exclaimed. "Do you know that she took 90% of that incentive money for the grant that we all worked on?"

I must say, I was not surprised to discover that a woman who (a) wanted to be added to research articles she didn't contribute to, (b) weaseled onto grant proposals she didn't work on (then took credit for acquiring the funds), (c) copied and pasted multiple documents, (d) harassed colleagues, (e) uttered the phrase "I gets grants," and (f) smugly exercised discourteous maliciousness as a quotidian habit—would assume the bulk of a cash grant incentive for herself despite not having an idea to contribute or writing a single sentence.

Honestly, she had proven herself to be a snake long before. Nevertheless, I had reached the apex of my vexation, and I wondered how the college president could allow such behavior. If you've ever come to the realization that someone has used you, it is a violation that hurts passed your skin.

I wasn't the only one who felt violated. Dissatisfaction grew among those who had written content and were going to implement the project-based work. The frustration reached the college president, and a conversation eventually occurred between him and me. It went something like this:

"Dr. Adder promotes a toxic environment, and this recent issue with the incentive for this grant is unethical," I said.

"Unethical?" was the president's reply. "There can only be one principal investigator."

"What?" my disdain spilled out disrespectfully. "That's not true," I continued in disbelief. "This is not a research grant, and what is she investigating? For that matter, she didn't do anything beyond schedule the Zoom meetings."

"Well, how would you have distributed the funds?" he asked.

"That's easy," I said, further dismayed by the question. "And I am actually surprised you even ask that. I would have distributed it evenly. Besides, that's what the policy indicates."

"What policy?" he asked.

"I spoke with the director of the office of research about it," I replied.

"Well, he doesn't know anything," the president responded.

At this point, I realized I was talking to Adder's master vampire or someone who had aligned himself with her for whatever reason. More akin to a good minion, he was doing her bidding. Though I knew it would be fruitless, I continued my futile protest.

"It's wrong, and how do you think any of us would ever react to working with her again?" I rhetorically asked.

"Well, she does what I want her to do," he defended and was done with the discussion.

Before this chat, I held the president in high regard, seeing him as a titan of ethics and good judgment. Imagine my shock when I had to reconcile my previous perception of him with this new one. Was my initial impression all a mask?

Weeks prior, I had made a request for $1,000 to buy books and journals for a budding student writing group. My request was met with silence—not, as I naïvely believed, because the coffers were bare, but seemingly because our literary ambitions didn't sparkle quite enough against the backdrop of bigger, flashier heists. Discovering that more than $40,000 was funneled toward an undeserving subordinate's (i.e., Adder) "incentive" made it clear; the creative aspirations of our students were merely background noise to the sweet symphony of pocket-lining at the top.

As for Adder's financial escapade? It swept through without consequence, leaving a trail of discontent in its wake, much like my forgotten request for $1,000—both buried and mourned in the same breath of institutional apathy. For the record, I used my own funds to buy those books.

In the case of this real-life scenario, the master vampire seems to be the college president himself. He gave Adder the permission—nay, the directive—to be a blood-sucking, shape-shifting narcissist. To use his words, "She does what I want her to do."

In a closer evaluation of the relationship between Adder and the college president, we can arrive at two plausible interpretations. First, it's conceivable that the president fell under the sway of Adder's hypnotic influence. This situation would render the president's role comparable to that of Renfield from Bram Stoker's *Dracula* (1931) and various adaptations. Renfield is the loyal servant to Count Dracula, often depicted as being under Dracula's control or influence. Van Wart et al. (2021) highlight that vampire leaders often wield hypnotic abilities to dominate and manipulate others to their advantage. Ideally, one would hope that presidents are immune to such undue influences, particularly those aimed at exploiting an institution for personal gain. Yet, the possibility remains.

Alternatively, it is easy for us to assume that an executive leader who permits vampiric behavior is a vampire leader as well. The senior leader often shares traits as equally telling, especially in the context of Twister's president. Acknowledging and justifying such behavior essentially equates to endorsement. The dynamic between Adder and the president—whether it involves Adder turning the president into a vampire or vice versa—remains ambiguous. Nonetheless, it underscores a critical point: leaders are accountable for their actions and, irrespective of their status, must ultimately answer to others, be it an individual or a group.

Adder had openly admitted that her goal was to become an institutional president; woe to the academic institution that puts her in charge. No doubt, it would become a snake pit.

For this scenario, this leader, who by virtue of her relationship with the president, willfully edifies herself through the efforts of others, taking credit for projects, tasks, and initiatives. Being in Adder's company was like being in a vampire's nest. While the folly may lie with the senior leader (i.e., the president of Twister College) who grants such unchecked autonomy, Adder is not excused for her villainy. A principled leader would never leverage that extension of power for personal gain, nor would he or she demonstrate such blatant disrespect by feeding off others' accomplishments and skill.

The ramifications of such behavior within an academic setting are far-reaching and detrimental. Trust among faculty, staff, and students is eroded. Individuals feel depleted because they are being used and not appreciated. Adder submitted the grant incentive document and included only her name on it, thus giving herself autonomy over the large cash incentive. Like other vampire leaders, she withheld key information, and power becomes concentrated in select hands. As a further outcome of vampire leaders, communication breaks down, fostering an environment of suspicion and mistrust. Institutional policies and decision-making processes become obscured, tarnishing the institution's reputation and leaving stakeholders confused, frustrated, and disenfranchised.

Partnerships break down. In the case of Adder, Take Flight Association indeed took flight from Twister. They abandoned the project which had the potential to promote growth for the college and opportunity for its students. There is no doubt that Adder is the reason the project did not materialize. The countenances of the association's representatives on that Zoom meeting leave no doubt in my mind.

Further negative outcomes from this type of centralized power often results in an unequal distribution of resources and opportunities, with those in positions of authority favoring certain individuals, breeding perceptions of favoritism and unfairness. Likewise, innovation and creativity suffer when decision-making is monopolized, stifling the free exchange of ideas that should be the lifeblood of any academic institution.

For me, working with Adder after the fiasco with the incentive was a tough for a while. Nothing about her changed; she behaved the same. The change took place in me. Drawing from Shirzad Chamine's Positive Intelligence, I explored three potential silver linings stemming from my encounters with the snake-headed, vampire-like leader: (1) I saw an opportunity to leverage these experiences and the outcomes to advocate for cultural, procedural, and policy shifts; (2) I viewed her behavior as a cautionary tale, providing valuable lessons on poor leadership; and (3) I recognized the chance to hone my skills in navigating challenging interpersonal dynamics. While these interpretations may not align precisely with Chamine's original concept of "positives," they represent the most constructive insights I could derive from the situation.

In environments plagued by bloodsuckers, it's crucial for principled leaders to illuminate the impact and consequences that arise when vampires lurk among us. The severed relationship between Twister and the Take Flight Association, resulting in a missed opportunity to expand enrollment, is just one example of the losses incurred due to Adder's influence. It's likely that other detrimental outcomes can be attributed to her actions as well.

When favoritism exists between vampire leaders and higher authorities, direct confrontation with the vampires themselves may prove unproductive. However, we cannot afford to turn a blind eye to the resulting impacts and outcomes. By shedding light on these outcomes, we pave the way for potential change. Institutions are obligated to report and justify their outcomes to accrediting bodies, alumni, partners, and boards. By focusing on the institutional impact rather than the personal behavior of vampire leaders, we increase the likelihood of eventual change.

While completely purging our institutions of such leaders may be an idealistic goal, we must strive to minimize their influence. Only then can an institution truly flourish and foster an environment characterized by trust, collaboration, and shared purpose—a stark contrast to the nightmarish realm inhabited by individuals like Adder, Twister's president, and their ilk.

Dark Reflections and Nightfall Scenarios

1. In the context of academic leadership, how do the dynamics of power and influence between a vampire leader and their master vampire (or enabler) affect the institution's culture and decision-making processes? Reflect on the ways these dynamics might obscure transparency and foster an environment of distrust and fear.
2. Scenario: You are a mid-level administrator at an academic institution where you have observed a senior leader, Dr. Adder, engaging

in manipulative and unethical behaviors, all while being protected and enabled by the college president.

- How would you document and address your concerns about Dr. Adder's behavior to ensure that they are taken seriously, considering the president's support for her actions?
- What strategies can you implement within your department to mitigate the negative impact of Dr. Adder's behavior on your team and maintain a culture of transparency and ethical leadership despite the broader institutional challenges?
- Reflect on your own leadership practices and consider any behaviors that might be perceived as toxic or manipulative by your colleagues. How can you identify and address these behaviors to ensure you are fostering a positive, supportive, and ethical environment for your team? What steps can you take to seek feedback and make necessary changes?

PART III

CHANGING THE DIRECTION OF THE BITE: WE BITE BACK

CALL TO ACTION

Reflecting on the experiences shared by the writers here, alongside the enigmatic characters like Nightshade and Dr. Adder, our aim is to illuminate the dark behaviors that lurk within academia. We are not naive; we recognize that these behaviors are not exclusive to academic leadership but can manifest in various realms, including families and other group settings. In this context, we hope that the insights gleaned from these stories are applicable beyond academia. Furthermore, we trust that the insights into their impacts, the recognition of underlying dispositions, and the proposed next steps in the forthcoming chapters will prove universally beneficial.

As we embark on the next phase of our journey, it is crucial to reflect on the lessons learned and chart a path forward. Change is attainable, but it demands courage, resilience, and an unwavering commitment to nurturing positive leadership practices.

In the upcoming chapters, we will delve into a real-world case study of organizational change, explore a framework for cultivating innovative leadership paradigms, and envision the characteristics of a university led by enlightened leaders. Through these explorations, we aim to pave the way for a brighter future for academia—one liberated from the shadows cast by vampire leaders and guided by the principles of integrity, collaboration, and shared purpose.

Let us draw strength from the wisdom gained from past experiences as we navigate the present challenges and shape the trajectory of academia for generations to come. Together, we can dispel the shadows and usher in a new era of leadership excellence.

CHAPTER 10

FROM THE ASHES: RADICAL REBIRTHS TO DEFY ANNIHILATION

Patrice W. Glenn Jones
Alabama State University, USA

Gary Shore's dark fantasy film *Dracula Untold* (2014) stands as one of our favorite vampire tales, although some may prefer the lighthearted charm of Adam Sandler's *Hotel Transylvania* series. In this grim narrative, Luke Evans portrays Prince Vlad Tepes, who embraces the monstrous form of a vampire and transforms into a figure feared by his own people—to obtain the power necessary to protect his family and kingdom from the looming threat of the Turkish Sultan.

Vlad's path toward the realm of the undead is paved with a haunting past. As a royal child ward of the Sultan, he earned the moniker "Vlad the Impaler, Son of the Dragon" after mercilessly slaughtering thousands and impaling them on spears. However, turning away from this brutal history, Vlad's realignment with the forces of death is fueled by a more personal stake—the new Turkish Sultan demands that Vlad's only son suffer the same fate of servitude that once befell Vlad himself.

Faced with the harrowing prospect of losing his child, Vlad embraces the monstrous powers of vampirism, not for personal gain or conquest, but as a sacrifice to protect his family and kingdom from the Sultan's tyranny. This transformation, while striking fear in his own subjects, is driven by a paternal love and a ruler's duty to safeguard his people, rendering Vlad a heroic, albeit fearsome, figure.

Vlald's rebirth as a creature of the night is a sacrifice of his humanity, undertaken to defeat a formidable foe and preserve the future of the next generation in his kingdom. Even before taking this intended temporary step toward vampirism, Prince Vlad is depicted as a confident; potentially narcissistic; yet loving ruler, husband, and father.

While some sociologists and psychologists might argue that narcissistic tendencies are inherent in human nature, we contend that Prince Vlad's degree of self-assurance does not equate to the self-serving motivations often associated with vampire leaders. Although confidence and charisma may present similarly on the surface, the underlying motives diverge. Vlad's actions stem from a place of selflessness, driven by a desire to safeguard his family and his kingdom's people, ultimately rendering him a heroic vampire figure.

In a loose parallel—go along with it—we encountered a real-life academic leader who embodied the spirit of Prince Vlad's heroic sacrifice. Prior to assuming the role of university president, Andrew Tepes was an elected official who left a legacy that converted relationships among those in his town. Though conceivably positive, Tepes' transformative practices were not always well received. He ruffled some feathers and made some enemies, but he also created alliances and forged a path for further improvements. Once his term was over, Tepes moved more into a role of advocacy. Driven by a deep love for his alma mater and a steadfast commitment to safeguarding its future, Tepes stepped forward to confront the formidable challenges threatening the very existence of the institution he held dear.

Much like Prince Vlad, who embraced the fearsome powers of a vampire to protect his kingdom, Tepes assumed a role that would require him to make difficult choices and confront daunting obstacles, all in service of preserving the institution and its community for generations to come.

Case Study

For years, a private liberal arts college in the northeastern United States grappled with a litany of challenges, including accreditation issues, budgetary fluctuations, mismanagement of talent, and dwindling enrollment numbers. A succession of presidents left the institution floundering, seemingly unable to steer it toward stability.

According to some accounts, certain chief leaders were consumed by self-motivation and personal interests that did not align with the institution's mission or its stakeholders' best interests. Based on those accounts, we image that those former presidents may have possessed vampiric qualities. The situation reached a critical juncture in the early 2000s when the college lost its accreditation due to allegations of plagiarism. The following year, the institution's appeal was denied, and it was only through federal litigation that the college could demonstrate it had been denied due process, ultimately leading to the restoration of its accreditation.

Over a decade, the institution underwent a consistent decline, and talks of an unavoidable closure ensued. That is, until a hero stepped in. President Tepes was an alumnus of the institution who initially assumed the executive leadership role in an interim capacity after having spent more time as an elected official.

Within months of assuming the temporary position, President Tepes was appointed as the permanent president. Characterized by strong business community ties, public prominence, management skills, and integrity, President Tepes demonstrated his commitment to the institution in many ways. He consistently expressed his commitment to the community and to preserving the legacy of the institution as well as charting a course for a productive future. President Tepes "put his money where his mouth was" in several ways. He fought to rid the institution of relationships that preyed on the institution's resources. This action transformed many "institutional allies" into foes. He also donated a significant portion of his salary back to the institution. Furthermore, he worked tirelessly foster buy in among the institutional staff which eventually led to increased enrollment and reciprocally beneficial relationships crucial to protecting the college's future.

Under his leadership, the institution underwent a remarkable transformation. Through fiscal management and strategic planning, two additional buildings were constructed, including a police substation with a student lab, and attractive academic programs were added to the college's offerings.

While some disagreed with President Tepes' tactics or decisions, perceiving them as not aligning with the institution's best interests, his primary concern was the well-being of the community rather than his perceived popularity. Some even criticized the president's professionalism. Ultimately, President Tepes' efforts turned the institution around, steering it toward a path of stability and growth.

Much like Prince Vlad in *Dracula Untold*, President Tepes embodied the archetype of a heroic figure willing to make sacrifices for the greater good of the community and the preservation of its future. While the film's portrayal of Vlad includes the archetypical elements of a vampire tale—the thirst for blood (which Vlad resists), the presence of a senior vampire, the turning of others into vampires, sensitivity to light, and even a minion character—Vlad's actions diverge from the typical vampire narrative. Unlike the self-serving motivations often associated with vampires, Vlad fires into action, sacrificing himself (no spoilers) to slay a more menacing threat, and to ensure the survival of his kingdom and its people—at least some of them. Loss certainly occurs, but a new dawn emerges from the ashes.

In an age marked by presidential attacks, chain reaction assaults on diversity, equity, access, inclusion, and curricula that make some uncomfortable, the academy and its leaders can draw inspiration from the examples set by

Prince Vlad and President Tepes. It is time for a new breed of transformative leaders to dawn in academia—leaders who channel the heroic spirit of these figures, willing to make difficult choices and sacrifices for the greater good of their institutions and the communities they serve.

Through their unwavering commitment, strategic vision, and selfless dedication, such leaders can navigate even the most formidable challenges, breathing new life into academic institutions and ensuring they remain beacons of learning, growth, and progress for generations to come.

Discussions and Actions

1. How can leaders in academia draw from the narrative of heroic sacrifice in *Dracula Untold* to balance the need for transformative change with ethical considerations, ensuring that their actions benefit the institution and its stakeholders rather than merely consolidating personal power?
2. Scenario: You have been appointed as the interim president of an academic institution facing significant challenges, including financial instability, declining enrollment, and low morale among faculty and staff. Drawing from the examples of Prince Vlad and President Tepes, outline your first 100-day action plan to begin the institution's radical rebirth.
    - How will you engage with various stakeholders to build trust and gather support for your initiatives?
    - What immediate steps will you take to address the financial and enrollment issues while fostering a positive and motivated institutional culture?
3. Reflect on your own leadership style and behaviors. Have there been instances where your actions could be perceived as self-serving or manipulative? How can you address these behaviors to ensure you are leading with integrity and prioritizing the well-being of your institution and its community?

CHAPTER 11

THE INFLUENCE OF LEADERSHIP

Patrice W. Glenn Jones
Alabama State University, USA

At this point, we will take a sabbatical from the examination of vampire leadership and our experiences with vampire leaders. We believe we've sufficiently shared encounters that give shape to this noxious, succubus-ian behavior. Now, our attention shifts to a discussion that amplifies why this book and the contents herein even matter. This chapter underscores the general importance of leadership, which has been discussed and argued for over a century. This discourse is not about whether leaders are born (i.e., trait) or made (i.e., situational) or the distinctions between leadership and management, as presented by Lawrence, Jr in this volume. This chapter also is not about the issues of gender, stereotypes, or leadership opportunities. Instead, this chapter provides practical discourse about leaders and how their influence on group behavior matters.

When it is all said and done, the reason leadership matters is because leaders lead groups. Groups of people can be effective and collaborative, or they can be dysfunctional and chaotically intertwined. The latter is what a good leader should aim to avoid.

I have not always had the awareness to be able to truly articulate why and how leadership matters, but like so many others, I have been infatuated with understanding leadership better. It was this desire that led me to investigate the dynamics of community and hope among K-12 leaders within African American schools (Jones, 2017). Though minimal, the positive relationship that I identified was enough for me to understand that values, emotions, and behaviors can act as a contagion. While my examination was only exploratory, other authors have examined how the values and behaviors of the leader thus can spread among his or her constituents.

In discussions of leadership styles, transformational leadership is often presented as an action of engendering significant changes in values and behaviors of their followers.

Transformational leadership is regularly viewed as positive, as the leader promotes positive changes in others, the group, and the institution. Burns (2012), however, has documented the use and misuse of leadership power throughout history. One person's idea of "transformation" could certainly be defined as an opposing behavior by another.

Avolio et al. (2014) researched leadership development and psychological mechanisms by which leadership behaviors are transmitted to and emulated by followers. For individuals with their own clearly defined values, a leader with opposing values can promote followers' detachment from a group. For others who are susceptible to the leader's personal values be it through manipulation, favor, or the desire for security, behavior adoption is likely. Again, leadership matters because leaders are community builders, or they can foster community fragmentation.

You certainly do not have to take my word on this. Various fields of study address group behavior influence. Let's start with the psychology of it all.

The Psychology of Group Behavior Influence

The influence of group behavior on individual actions is a well-established concepted in psychology. Social Learning Theory and Conformity are two theories that offer relevant perspectives on how behaviors are adopted, adjusted, or altered in group settings. The psychological explanation considers what occurs in the brain as will be smized here.

Social Learning Theory. As a child, your parent may have told you "Do as I say, not as I do" when you questioned why they could engage in certain behaviors that were alluring to you but disallowed your participation. The directive to behave a certain way, or in this case "not to do," is not an exclusive influencer of behavior.

Developed by Albert Bandura, Social Learning Theory suggests that individual acquire new behaviors through the processes of observation, imitation, and modeling, rather than solely through personal experience and direct reinforcement (Bandura, 1977). Understanding what happens in the brain during social learning involves examining various neural networks and brain structures that are activated.

The initial step in Social Learning is observation, where an individual notices the actions of another person. The *superior temporal sulcus* and the *parietal cortex* are critical areas involved in perceiving and paying attention to these actions (Gazzola et al., 2007). These brain regions help to focus attention on relevant stimuli and are crucial for recognizing and processing the movements and intentions of others.

One of the most significant discoveries related to Social Learning is the role of mirror neurons, which are found in regions such as the inferior frontal gyrus and premotor cortex (Rizzolatti & Craighero, 2004). Mirror neurons fire when an individual performs an action and when they observe the same action performed by someone else. This mirroring process helps the observer understand the action and its purpose, essentially allowing them to simulate the observed behavior internally without performing it.

Understanding and relating to the emotional state of others is crucial in social learning, especially when learning behaviors that involve social interactions or emotional responses. The *amygdala* and the *anterior insula* are key regions involved in processing emotions and empathy (Singer, 2006). These areas help individuals connect emotionally with what they observe, which can be crucial for motivation and the deeper learning of social norms and behaviors.

What continuous to occur in the brain is a sophisticated process involving different areas of the brain. Ultimately, Social Learning theory and what happens in the brain highlight that much of human learning is vicarious; we learn from seeing the outcomes of others' behaviors. For instance, in organizational contexts, when employees observe that proactive contributions are met with rewards, they are likely to emulate this behavior, aiming to receive similar recognition (Bandura, 1986). Emulation, or the continuation of a behavior through group influence, is easy enough to accept when the behavior does not contradict an individual's personal values. However, this is where Conformity comes in.

Conformity. Explored by Solomon Asch, Conformity is a psychology phenomenon that causes individuals to conform to a group norm even when the behavior or value contradicts their own senses (Asch, 1956). This tendency stems from the desire to fit into a group and avoid the discomfort for standing out. Conformity indicates that both real and perceived pressures can dramatically sway an individual's behaviors and beliefs.

The initial step in conformity often involves perceiving the behaviors and attitudes of others in a group. The brain actively processes social cues and non-verbal signals to assess group norms and expectations. According to social comparison theory, individuals evaluate their opinions and abilities by comparing themselves to others, especially in ambiguous situations. This comparison can lead to a reassessment of one's own beliefs if they appear to diverge from the group's beliefs.

When an individual's beliefs do not match their actions, it creates cognitive dissonance—a state of mental discomfort. The brain seeks to resolve this dissonance either by changing beliefs to align with the actions of the group or leader, or by rationalizing the behavior. This psychological discomfort is a significant motivator for changing either perceptions or behaviors to restore cognitive harmony. Cognitive dissonance leads individuals to either change their internal beliefs to match their external behaviors (thus reducing dissonance) or to justify their conformity by minimizing the importance of the discrepancy.

Conformity can also reinforce or alter a person's social identity. Aligning with group norms can strengthen an individual's identification with the group, enhancing his or her sense of belonging and self-esteem. Conversely, if conformity leads to negative outcomes, it can damage self-perception or lead to regret or self-criticism.

In practice, such as during team decision-making, even if an individual disagrees with a group's stances, he or she may still agree with the popular opinion to avoid conflict or alienation. When the relationship is hierarchical (i.e., leader to constituents) the potential for individual to resist leader alienation or to agree for favor is far more likely than with a parallel or horizontal relationship structure. Some people with "go along to get along" even when their values and thoughts converge.

The Sociology of Group Behavior Influence

In the field of sociology, group behavior influence explains how individual actions are shaped by larger social dynamics. This influence is particularly evident in the context of higher education, where leadership plays a critical role in guiding student behavior and shaping institutional culture. Sociological concepts such as social influence, group norms, and reference groups provide valuable frameworks to further understand the dynamics of group behavior influence.

Social Influence. Social Influence in higher education is multifaceted, encompassing conformity, compliance, and obedience, which are central to how students and faculty interact within the university setting. For example, a university president's approach to campus policies can significantly influence how administrators enforce these rules and how compliant students and faculty are. As Kiesler and Kiesler (1969) discuss in their exploration of conformity, the subtle pressures of wanting to align with university policies or the broader campus culture can lead students to conform to behaviors and ideologies that are endorsed by the institution. This type of social influence can be observed during orientations or ethical training sessions, where the emphasis on certain behaviors sets expectations for new students and staff.

Group Norms. Group Norms are another crucial element in higher education. These norms often manifest as unwritten rules that guide behavior on campus. They are observed in study habits, participation in student organizations, or interaction in social spaces, and are reinforced by peer interactions and expectations set by group leaders, such as resident advisors or club presidents. According to Feldman (1984), norms within university settings not only promote order but also ensure a sense of community and belonging among students. Leaders in higher education play a pivotal role in establishing these norms by modeling behaviors and explicitly stating what is expected of students and faculty, thereby guiding the group toward desired standards.

Reference Groups. Reference Groups function as benchmarks for individuals in assessing their own behaviors and aspirations. In higher education, these groups might include particular peer groups, academic departments, or even alumni networks that current students look up to. Students often emulate the behaviors, academic pursuits, or career paths of these groups. Vaughan and Hogg (2005) highlight the significance of reference groups in shaping individual identity within a group setting, such as a university. The influence of these groups is profound; they help students determine not only their social and academic behaviors but also their broader personal and professional goals.

Leadership within higher education institutions harnesses these sociological constructs to shape the campus environment and influence student behavior effectively. By understanding and applying the principles of social influence, group norms, and reference groups, leaders can create a positive campus culture that encourages academic excellence and personal development. Furthermore, effective leaders use these sociological insights to implement policies and initiatives that resonate with both the individual and collective aspirations of the university community, ensuring that the institution remains a vibrant and cohesive academic and social environment.

From Theory to Practice: Leadership in Education and the Pygmalion Effect

In higher education, leadership extends beyond administrative duties and is a critical driver of institutional ethos and educational quality. Leadership in education extends beyond the action of guiding. It must transform and build; it must also inspire. From the educational landscape, the Pygmalion Effect is particularly relevant theory to further understand the impact leaders have on constituents.

The Pygmalion Effect, also known as the self-fulfilling prophecy or the Rosenthal effect, is a psychological phenomenon whereby higher expectations lead to an increase in performance. First introduced by Robert K. Merton in 1948, the concept draws inspiration from the myth of Pygmalion, a sculptor in Greek mythology who fell in love with a statue he created and, through his adoration and expectation, brought it to life.

In exploring the Pygmalion effect within educational contexts, it becomes evident that the expectations teachers and leaders hold for their students or followers can profoundly shape their performance and outcomes (Rosenthal & Jacobson, 1968). This phenomenon is particularly salient in educational settings, where the beliefs and behaviors of teachers and leaders play a critical role in influencing students' beliefs, behaviors, and achievements (Jussim & Harber, 2005).

Teachers and leaders who maintain high expectations for their students or followers often demonstrate behaviors that align with these expectations (Eden, 1992). Their confidence in their students' or followers' potential and abilities informs their interactions and the opportunities they provide (Hattie & Timperley, 2007). For instance, a teacher who firmly believes in the capabilities of all her students is more likely to offer additional support and encouragement to help them realize their full potential.

The manner in which teachers and leaders communicate with their students or followers can significantly be influenced by their personal beliefs, which, in turn, can influence others' beliefs. Positive and affirming feedback can bolster individuals' confidence and self-efficacy, resulting in improved performance (Eccles et al., 1993). Conversely, negative or discouraging feedback can erode individuals' confidence and motivation, leading to diminished performance outcomes (Babad, 1995).

Teachers and leaders serve as role models for their students or followers, and their behaviors and actions can shape others' beliefs and expectations (Bandura, 1977). When teachers and leaders demonstrate unwavering confidence in their students' or followers' abilities and provide consistent support and encouragement, they set a powerful example that fosters a culture of high expectations and achievement (Seligman, 1998).

Moreover, the values, beliefs, and personal behaviors exhibited by teachers and leaders can be contagious and exert a profound influence on how others like students conceptualize their own abilities, as well as outcomes among other staff members in higher education, faculty, and learners (Rosenholtz & Simpson, 1984). By cultivating an environment characterized by high expectations, positive reinforcement, and personalized support, teachers and leaders can empower their students or followers to reach their full potential and achieve success (Leithwood & Jantzi, 2008).

In essence, the Pygmalion Effect underscores the pivotal role played by teachers' and leaders' values, beliefs, and personal behaviors in shaping the beliefs and expectations of others within educational settings. By fostering a positive and supportive environment grounded in high expectations, leaders can create conditions conducive to enhanced performance and success among their staff and learners (Hallinger & Heck, 1996). University leaders who expect great intellectual achievements and moral integrity from their students foster an environment where such outcomes are more attainable. How then, can a leader who does not have a personal sense of moral integrity foster such among stakeholders? How would it be possible for a vampire leader, for example, to architect and construct a thriving academic ecosystem where most people feel empowered, supported, and appreciated? Dare we say, such a leader cannot.

Discussions and Actions

Reflect on the impact of leadership, whether positive or negative, on your personal or professional life by writing a letter to a leader who has influenced you. This letter is a personal exercise meant for self-reflection and growth. You may choose to keep the letter private or send it to the leader; the choice is yours.

Reflective Prompts for Writing the Letter:

1. *Identifying Impactful Moments:*
   - Think of a specific moment when the leader's actions or decisions significantly influenced you. What happened, and how did it make you feel?
2. *Analyzing Leadership Style:*
   - Consider the leader's overall approach to leadership. Were they transformational, transactional, or perhaps a mix of styles? How did their style align with or differ from your own values?
3. *Personal Growth and Learning:*
   - Reflect on how these experiences have influenced your personal and professional growth. What have you learned about effective leadership, and how have you applied these lessons in your current role?
4. *Expressing Gratitude:*
   - Regardless of the nature of the leader's impact, express gratitude for the lessons learned.

     "How has their influence contributed to your development and understanding of leadership?" By completing this task, you will gain deeper insights into the profound impact of leadership on individuals and groups. This reflective exercise will also help you identify key elements of effective leadership that you can apply in your own practice.

CHAPTER 12

CREATING "A SPACE" FOR NEW LEADERSHIP: COURAGEOUS LEADERSHIP FOR ADAPTIVE CHANGE

Patrice W. Glenn Jones
Alabama State University, USA

It takes courage to follow the advice of Warren Bennis (2000) who wrote, "Leaders must encourage their organizations to dance to forms of music yet to be heard" (p. 34). Many of the world's most celebrated leaders were once looked at as eccentric personalities who stood alone and danced to a different beat. As we examine the current state of higher education and anticipate the uncertain future, we are in need of leaders who not only dance to a different beat but who also create the beat. Beyond courage, dancing to unproduced music requires innovation, adaptability, and vision.

During the 20232024 American Council on Education fellowship experience, some fellows took every opportunity afforded to ask presidents, other executive leaders, colleagues, cohort members, and others a simple yet crucial question: *With consideration for today's educational landscape and with respect for this uncertain future, what qualities does an executive leader in higher education need?* Most respondents were not at a lost to provide responses.

Data from 73 respondents was collected. Of the respondents, 11 were college or university presidents or chancellors. From October of 2023 to June on 2024, 281 phrases of data, some of which were duplications, were collected. The goal of the posed question was to identify common themes in the qualities of necessary leadership. From the data, a leadership framework was developed. It marks the dawning of new leadership, one that represents—hopefully—an antitheist or nemesis of vampire leadership.

Vampire Leaders Don't Nurture

The parasitic nature of vampire leadership, characterized by its draining impact, at this point should be recognized as a detriment to colleges and universities. This type of leadership is particularly harmful to academic institutions already facing financial difficulties. Draining resources from institutions that are already financially vulnerable could potentially lead to their closure. Referencing the title of this volume, it is crucial to consider the fundamental meaning of "sucking"—essentially, it denotes extraction or depletion. The antithesis of this would be to invest in or nurture these institutions.

In light-hearted terms, if vampire leadership is akin to a never-ending series of horror flicks where the characters never really learn or grow, nurturing leadership is more of a nurturing nature documentary, where the ecosystem flourishes and each species—no matter how small—plays a pivotal role in the health of the environment.

Nurturing Leadership

Some years ago, Williams et al. (2008) examined the role of nurturing as a quality of advising that often occurs at small institutions and those who serve high numbers of students of color (e.g., minority-serving and historically Black institutions).

> At these institutions, many students look upon instructors and college personnel as "family." The students develop a territorial protectiveness and appreciation for college personnel who show them they care. For many HBCU employees, their career is more than a job; it is a service to the black community. Black colleges nurture black students. (Williams et al., 2008, para. 2)

The concept of nurtured advising has evolved into a focus on nurturing as a leadership. While leadership in industry is often drive by profits and profit margins, leadership in education, though it considers revenue, is fundamentally about people. Moreover, young people and learners are at the center of the educational ecosystem. Therefore, it is crucial that educational leaders are ethical. Educational leaders should enact positive changes and lead stakeholders to a vision of academic achievement.

More than any other area of leadership, educational leadership requires degrees of empathy, giving, and vision. Educational leaders must "pour into" colleagues, constituents, potential partners, industrial leaders, donors, students, faculty, staff, and the communities they represent.

Nurtured leadership has been discussed by various authors (e.g., Hashimy et al., 2023; Jones, 2016; Muñoz et al., 2018). According to Jones (2016), who contributed to the Nurtured Advising framework, nurturing leadership is marked by mentorship and nurturing as the primary characteristics. Nurturing leaders are also characterized by humility, willingness to incorporate humor, and passion—not only for the vision or the institution but for the people in the institution. Ultimately, nurturing leaders pour into stakeholders and the institutions they represent.

Nurturing leaders are also protective, similar to the way a mother would protect her children or a father would protect his family. They encourage senior followers to nurture others through mentorship. This form of leadership is well-suited to educational institutions, family-centered organizations, and organizations where education is a primary focus.

At its core, nurturing leadership involves a generous watering of encouragement and a steady fertilization of support which foster an academic ecosystem that thrives on the mutual benefits of shared knowledge and respect. Where vampire leaders may hoard information and expertise—sinking their teeth into the jugular of creativity—nurturing leaders distribute these resources liberally to ensure that every corner of their institution is lush with potential and vibrant with diversity.

The shift from a bloodletting paradigm to one of nurturing might initially unnerve those more accustomed to the gothic arches of traditional power structures. However, the transition is less about overthrowing the old guard and more about reinvigorating the landscape. It is about replacing the cloak of secrecy with the transparency of a greenhouse, where every seed has a chance to grow, and every plant can reach toward the sun.

Nurturing leadership contrasts with vampire leadership and precedes the leadership framework that emerged from the data collected among the respondents.

The Identified Themes

In isolating themes collected from among the data of 73 respondents, organized by thematic analysis, a standard qualitative process was followed. However, qualitative software was not used. The data was read and reviewed several times by three individuals—the data collector and two outsiders. Similar ideas were noted.

The data was coded using basic methods, which involved highlighting and annotating repeating patterns. The themes were reviewed multiple times. They were checked to determine if the themes worked in relation to the coded extracts (Level 1) and the entire data set (Level 2). Some themes merged while others diverged. Thus, the initial categorization among the datum were identified. After refining each theme and the overall story the analysis conveys, final names for each theme were identified. The themes reflect the essence of what each theme captures about the data. Six themes were identified (See Table 12.1).

In the evolving landscape of higher education, traditional leadership models often fall short in addressing the rapid changes and diverse challenges. The themes are not new, but in light of the vampires among the academy, the interdependence of the themes reflects a need for a leadership approach that effectively occupies "A SPACE"—a metaphorical realm where agility meets vision and ethics meets empowerment. "A SPACE" is also an acronym representing the themes of adaptive, courageous leadership.

Table 12.1

Leadership Themes and Qualities

Themes	Leadership Qualities
Agile resilience	Resilience, minimizing cost of mistakes, adaptability, spine for leading change
Principled influence	Political savviness, exit strategy planning, personal sacrifice, moral reasoning, selflessness, influencing kindness, operational integrity, honesty, confident humility, appropriate situational transparency, love of learning and life-long learner, commitment to mentorship
Compassionate connectivity	Empathy, fueling creativity and satisfaction, relationship building, prioritizes people, curiosity and listening, community-focused decisions, transparent communication, making people feel special, giving everyone a voice, likability, shows appreciation, nurtures the collective, exalts others, considers stakeholder satisfaction; global competency
Strategic visionary	Vision-centered, courage to innovate, willing to break convention, tech comfort and curiosity, forward-thinking, tech literacy, risk management, purposeful decision making, strategic thinking, leading change, prioritizing institutional needs, builds strong teams; high degree of discernment, uses influences responsibility, solution-oriented
Authentic empowerment	Personal values in leadership, self-awareness, expansive thinking, inclusive winning attitude, continuous learning, cultivating growth in others, authentic confidence, courage and conviction, creativity, fostering team spirit, empowers others; creates a culture of shared ideas
Entrepreneurial fiscal stewardship	Entrepreneurial, fiscal responsibility, financial knowledge and planning, understands the impact of giving, fiscal trustworthiness; plan for multiple revenue steams

Courageous Leadership for Adaptive Change

The Courageous Leadership for Adaptive Change (CLAC) framework offers a refreshing and powerful alternative to vampire leadership styles that drain innovation and motivation with their antiquated methods. "A SPACE" in this context is not just a physical dimension but a strategic expanse filled with the qualities essential for leading modern educational institutions into the future:

- *A* for *Agile Resilience*: In the face of global challenges and unexpected crises, agile resilience allows leaders to pivot quickly and ensures that institutions not only survive but thrive through adversity.
- *S* for *Strategic Visionary*: Looking beyond the immediate, strategic visionaries map out long-term goals that anticipate future educational needs and technological advancements. They craft pathways that lead toward groundbreaking achievements.
- *P* for *Principled Influence*: Rooted in ethical leadership, principled influence fosters a culture of integrity and fairness, crucial in an era where stakeholders from students to staff demand transparency and ethical decision-making.
- *A* for *Authentic Empowerment*: True leadership empowers all echelons of the institution, from administrators to academics and encourages a participatory culture where every voice is valued, and every individual feels motivated to contribute their best.
- *C* for *Compassionate Connectivity*: Compassionate connectivity underscores the significance of empathy and understanding in leadership. It's about building bridges between diverse groups, nurturing relationships that are grounded in mutual respect and understanding, as well as enhancing the collaborative spirit within and outside the organization.
- *E* for *Entrepreneurial Fiscal Stewardship*: Combining fiscal prudence with entrepreneurial spirit, this trait ensures that institutions not only manage their budgets wisely but also innovate new revenue streams that support sustainable growth.

Agile Resilience

"Agile Resilience" is a central theme in higher education leadership, particularly within the CLAC framework. Observations of current leadership trends reveal that this quality transcends mere survival of setbacks, encapsulating the foresight and strategic planning essential for minimizing risks and reducing costs. Agile resilience is fundamentally about dynamically responding to challenges and continuously adapting to shifting circumstances, ensuring that educational institutions not only endure but also thrive in an ever-changing landscape.

Leaders who embody agile resilience are marked by their exceptional flexibility and profound resolve, qualities crucial for effectively navigating and managing transformative changes. This capability becomes increasingly critical as institutions face the rapid evolution of technology, unpredictable global events, and shifting societal needs, all of which pose significant challenges to the stability and growth of academic environments.

For example, imagine a university leader who quickly implements hybrid learning models in response to sudden public health guidelines changes. This leader ensures the infrastructure accommodates both online and in-person learning and takes the opportunity to reevaluate the curriculum to enhance the use of digital tools. Such adaptability not only addresses immediate logistical challenges but also sets a precedent for future flexibility in educational delivery, significantly bolstering the institution's resilience.

In another scenario, a university might proactively guard against financial instability by diversifying its revenue streams, forming innovative partnerships with technology companies and local businesses. This strategy not only protects the institution from fluctuations in traditional funding sources like tuition fees and government grants but also exemplifies agile resilience. It shows how strategic foresight and proactive planning are vital for maintaining operations and driving growth.

The value of agile resilience in higher education is immense. It compels leaders to navigate uncertainty with steadiness, sparks innovative problem-solving, and cultivates a proactive, strategic institutional culture. By fostering agile resilience, leaders ensure their institutions are well-equipped to face the future, continuously innovate, and adapt to the ever-evolving demands of global education.

Strategic Visionary

"Strategic Visionary" emerges as the second pivotal theme from respondent feedback within the CLAC framework. Observations from higher education highlight that strategic visionaries possess a crucial ability to look beyond current challenges and to leverage innovation as well as forward-thinking to spearhead transformative changes. This leadership theme emphasizes the essential ability of leaders to extend their gaze beyond the immediate horizon, channeling their vision into strategic, long-term initiatives that significantly shape the direction of their institutions. Strategic visionaries in higher education are especially notable for their readiness to embrace new technologies, challenge existing academic conventions, and guide their institutions through transformative changes that anticipate the future of education.

A quintessential example of such leadership could involve a university president who, recognizing the rapid evolution of digital technology and its impact on learning modalities, spearheads the creation of an immersive virtual reality campus. This initiative would not only revolutionize how students engage with their studies but also establish the institution as a leader in educational innovation. By doing so, the leader demonstrates not just tech literacy but a forward-thinking mindset that integrates technology to enhance educational outcomes.

Another scenario might feature a dean who introduces a cross-disciplinary program that combines artificial intelligence, ethics, and environmental science. This program, developed in response to global demands for sustainable practices and responsible artificial intelligence use, showcases the leader's vision-centered approach and courage to innovate. It also reflects strategic thinking and purposeful decision-making, as the program directly addresses emerging global challenges while positioning the university at the cutting edge of academic and research excellence.

Strategic visionary leaders are also characterized by their strong risk management skills. For instance, consider a scenario where a provost implements a sophisticated data analytics system to predict enrollment trends and financial forecasts. This system allows the institution to manage its resources more effectively, minimizing financial risks and ensuring stability even in uncertain times.

Moreover, the ability to build strong teams is central to the strategic visionary theme. A leader might cultivate a team dedicated to integrating artificial intelligence across the curriculum, ensuring that the institution not only keeps pace with technological advancements but also leads in developing new educational paradigms. This task force would embody the leader's commitment to robust team-building and solution-oriented outcomes.

Principled Influence

The "Principled Influence" theme emphasizes a leadership style marked by ethical fortitude, strategic foresight, and a deep commitment to the welfare of others. This approach underscores the importance of navigating organizational politics with integrity, planning for contingencies with wisdom, and making personal sacrifices for the greater good. Leaders embodying this theme are characterized by their moral reasoning, selflessness, and a genuine concern for the impact of their actions on people and the organization. They prioritize honesty and transparency, adjust their openness to suit the situation, and foster a culture of kindness and learning within their teams.

Leaders who exemplify principled influence are distinguished by their robust moral reasoning, selflessness, and deep concern for the effects of their actions on both individuals and the broader organization. They are committed to honesty and transparency and skillfully adjust their openness to fit various situations. Thereby, these leaders foster an environment where kindness and lifelong learning flourish among their teams.

For instance, imagine a university chancellor who, recognizing the potential financial challenges ahead, proactively engages in exit strategy planning to safeguard the institution's future. This chancellor might establish an emergency fund that supports both academic programs and student scholarships in times of fiscal downturns. In doing such, this leader does not just illustrate foresight but also displays commitment to operational integrity and the educational mission.

Another example could be a dean who demonstrates political savviness and confident humility by spearheading a campus-wide initiative to integrate more inclusive practices. Understanding the delicate balance of internal politics, this dean navigates through bureaucratic hurdles and potential resistance by transparently communicating the benefits and soliciting broad input, thereby ensuring buy-in and fostering a culture of inclusivity.

Moreover, principled leaders in higher education might show a love of learning and commitment to mentorship by setting up mentorship programs that not only support young faculty and administrators but also encourage seasoned professionals to engage in continuous professional development. This initiative not only enhances personal and professional growth but also strengthens the institution's academic community.

In emphasizing the importance of agile resilience, these examples of principled influence underscore how ethical leadership is not static but dynamically adapts to changing circumstances and challenges. By adhering to their principles, leaders not only navigate complex scenarios with grace but also inspire their institutions to emerge stronger and more cohesive in the face of adversity

Thus, "Principled Influence" in the context of higher education leadership is essential for fostering an ethical, transparent, and resilient academic environment. It encourages leaders to remain steadfast in their values while innovatively responding to the evolving educational landscape, thereby ensuring that their institutions not only survive but thrive.

Authentic Empowerment

"Authentic Empowerment" emerges as the fourth theme among the respondents in our exploration of the CLAC framework in higher education. This theme celebrates leadership that is deeply anchored in strong personal values and self-awareness, and it underscores a leadership approach committed to cultivating an inclusive and creatively stimulating team environment.

Leaders who champion this theme recognize and leverage their strengths and those of others. However, they also enthusiastically embrace the expansion of their horizons through continuous learning, collaboration, a sincere desire to promote individual and collective growth, along with innovative thinking.

Leaders who embody "Authentic Empowerment" play a pivotal role in inspiring both confidence and empowerment within their teams. They give others the permission to be change agents, innovators, and even disrupters if these roles are for the advancement of the institution. They foster a culture ripe with shared ideas and drive growth by nurturing the potential in others, making their institutions not just centers of learning but hubs of innovation and creativity.

Consider a fictional scenario in which a university president, renowned for her expansive thinking and inclusive winning attitude, launches an "Innovation Incubator" for students and faculty across all disciplines. This initiative provides resources, mentorship, and support for turning creative ideas into tangible projects or startups. Here, the leader's commitment to empowering others shines brightly, as does her dedication to creating a nurturing environment that values diverse perspectives and collaboration.

Another example might involve a dean who embodies authentic empowerment by implementing a professional development program tailored specifically for administrative staff. This program focuses on leadership skills, project management, and effective communication. The program's focuses illustrate that the dean's understanding that empowering all levels of staff is crucial for the overall health and success of the institution. This initiative not only boosts morale but also enhances operational efficiency and service delivery across the campus.

Congruent with the agile resilience theme, these examples of authentic empowerment underscore how essential it is for leaders to adapt and respond to the needs of their community dynamically by fostering capacity. Leaders practicing authentic empowerment do not rigidly stick to traditional methods but are flexible and open to adopting new approaches that better serve their evolving institutions.

Thus, "Authentic Empowerment" within higher education leadership provides a hopeful and effective tenet for fostering an environment where every member of the institution feels valued, capable, and inspired. It encourages leaders to remain true to their values while continually seeking ways to innovate and improve, ensuring that their institutions are not only adaptive and resilient but also thriving and forward-thinking communities.

Compassionate Connectivity

"Compassionate Connectivity" stands out as the fifth key theme. This theme is characterized by deep-rooted empathy, open communication, and a steadfast commitment to engaging with both the community and stakeholders. It underscores a leadership approach that nurtures creativity, ensures inclusivity, and builds robust, enduring relationships across and beyond the institution. Leaders who champion this theme excel at making every individual—whether student, staff, or faculty—feel truly valued and heard, thus fostering a positive organizational culture that prioritizes satisfaction and appreciation.

Imagine a university leader who introduces a "Campus Voices" initiative, a monthly forum designed to provide all members of the university community—from grounds staff to tenured professors—the opportunity to share their ideas and concerns directly with the administration. This leader ensures that these sessions are not just symbolic but lead to actionable outcomes, thereby fostering a sense of inclusivity and participation. Such an initiative not only demonstrates transparent communication but also significantly boosts morale and nurtures the collective spirit of the campus.

In another example, consider a college president who establishes an annual "Global Days" event that celebrates the diverse cultures represented on campus. This event includes workshops, panels, and festivities, which are not only fun but also educational, enhancing global competency and understanding among students and staff. This effort goes beyond mere relationship building; it embeds a deep respect for cultural diversity within the fabric of the institution's everyday life.

Moreover, leaders dedicated to compassionate connectivity might implement mentoring programs that pair incoming international students with local students to help them navigate the challenges of adapting to a new environment. Such programs are grounded in empathy and a genuine desire to ensure that every student not only succeeds academically but also feels welcomed and supported.

The importance of compassionate connectivity in higher education cannot be overstated. It compels leaders to prioritize people, listen with curiosity, and make community-focused decisions that enhance the educational experience for everyone involved. By fostering this kind of connectivity, leaders not only build a more supportive and collaborative academic community but also prepare their institutions to meet the challenges of a globalized world with competence and compassion.

Thus, leaders who practice "Compassionate Connectivity" are not just administrators; they are pivotal social architects who recognize the value of every community member and are committed to building a more inclusive, engaged, and satisfied academic environment.

Entrepreneurial Financial Stewardship

"Entrepreneurial Financial Stewardship" emerges as a critical final theme. This leadership trait skillfully melds innovative and entrepreneurial thinking with stringent financial management and planning. This approach emphasizes the necessity for leaders to be both proactive and creative in their financial strategies while upholding the highest standards of fiscal responsibility and transparency.

Consider a hypothetical scenario where a university president, renowned for her entrepreneurial spirit, spearheads the development of a corporate partnership program. This initiative involves collaborating with major technology firms to fund research and development centers on campus. These centers not only provide students with access to cutting-edge technology and invaluable hands-on experience but also open new revenue streams for the university. The president's strategic vision in establishing these partnerships exemplifies fiscal responsibility and an entrepreneurial approach to financial planning.

Another example could involve a college dean who implements a unique alumni funding model that encourages recent graduates to invest in campus startups in exchange for small equity stakes. This innovative financial strategy not only fosters a spirit of entrepreneurship within the student body but also strengthens ties with alumni, who become directly engaged in the institution's ongoing success and innovation. The dean's initiative showcases an understanding of the strategic value of giving and aligns alumni interests with the university's growth, reinforcing fiscal trustworthiness and commitment to community impact.

Moreover, leaders committed to Entrepreneurial Financial Stewardship might launch sustainability initiatives that reduce operational costs while enhancing the institution's environmental and social impact. For instance, investing in green campus infrastructure projects like solar power installations or energy-efficient buildings not only cuts long-term energy costs but also attracts grants and donations from environmentally conscious organizations. This approach not only exemplifies fiscal responsibility but also positions the institution as a leader in sustainability, appealing to prospective students and faculty who prioritize environmental issues.

The significance of Entrepreneurial Financial Stewardship in higher education leadership is profound. It compels leaders to think outside traditional funding models, engage in rigorous financial planning, and explore creative avenues for financial sustainability. By integrating entrepreneurial approaches with meticulous financial oversight, leaders not only secure their institutions' financial health but also champion innovative practices that can lead to substantial community and educational benefits.

The Takeaway

Change is one of the only constants in the world, and nowhere is this more evident than in the realm of academia. As educational institutions navigate through the complexities of technological advances, cultural shifts, and global challenges, the necessity for adaptive and visionary leadership becomes paramount. The model of CLAC emerges as a vital alternative to the extractive practices of vampire leadership, which drain institutions of their vitality and impede progressive development.

This dynamic leadership framework is underpinned by the connective power of its six core tenets, which collectively take up "A SPACE" in the academic leadership landscape. This initialism—standing for Agile Resilience, Strategic Visionary, Principled Influence, Authentic Empowerment, Compassionate Connectivity, and Entrepreneurial Financial Stewardship—represents a holistic approach to leading institutions through periods of uncertainty and transformation. Each component is crucial in fostering an environment where innovation, inclusivity, and forward-thinking are not just encouraged but are fundamentally integrated into the fabric of the institution.

"A SPACE" delineates a leadership approach that is both responsive and responsible. Agile Resilience ensures that institutions can swiftly adapt to changing circumstances without losing sight of their long-term goals. A leader who is a Strategic Visionary stretches beyond current challenges to anticipate future needs and opportunities. Principled Influence fosters a culture of integrity and ethical decision-making that builds trust and respect across all levels of the organization. Authentic Empowerment champions the growth and development of every community member, facilitating a shared sense of purpose and achievement.

Furthermore, Compassionate Connectivity emphasizes the importance of empathy and open communication, which are essential for creating a supportive and collaborative academic community. Finally, Entrepreneurial Financial Stewardship equips leaders with the skills to navigate fiscal challenges innovatively and sustainably, ensuring that institutions not only survive financial vicissitudes but also thrive and expand their impact.

CLAC provides a comprehensive framework for academic leaders who are ready to move beyond the confines of traditional leadership models. It offers a strategic, empathetic, and principled approach that aligns with the evolving demands of global higher education. By embracing "A SPACE," leaders can ensure that their institutions are well-equipped to face the future, marked by a commitment to growth, inclusivity, and resilience. This is the kind of leadership that dances to unheard music and that does not just occupy a space. This leadership transforms it.

Discussions and Actions

1. Reflect on Your Leadership Impact: Consider your current leadership style and its impact on your organization or team. How do you see yourself embodying the qualities of agile resilience,

principled influence, compassionate connectivity, or other themes from the "A SPACE" framework? What changes could you make to better align with these transformative leadership qualities?
2. Scenario Exercise: Imagine you are the new president of a struggling university that has seen a decline in enrollment and a drop in staff morale. Using the "A SPACE" framework, outline a strategic initiative to turn the institution around.

Details:

- *Agile Resilience:* How will you quickly adapt to the changing educational landscape?
- *Strategic Visionary:* What is your long-term vision for the university, and how will you inspire others to share this vision?
- *Principled Influence:* How will you ensure ethical decision-making and integrity in your leadership?
- *Authentic Empowerment:* What steps will you take to empower faculty, staff, and students?
- *Compassionate Connectivity:* How will you build strong, empathetic relationships within the university community?
- *Entrepreneurial Financial Stewardship:* What innovative financial strategies will you employ to stabilize and grow the university's finances?

CHAPTER 13

THE COLLEGE OF TOMORROW: GUIDED BY COURAGEOUS LEADERSHIP FOR ADAPTIVE CHANGE

Patrice W. Glenn Jones
Alabama State University, USA

Imagine stepping onto the campus of a university that's not just a place of learning, but a dynamic ecosystem where every person, from the janitor to the president, feels indispensable. The aesthetic of such a campus would obviously match the culture and climate that looms with a verbosity that unearths talents and empowers the unlikely.

As you step onto the campus, the first thing that catches your eye is the stunning blend of natural beauty and modern innovation. The landscape is meticulously designed, with verdant lawns and gardens featuring a plethora of native plants that bloom in vibrant colors year-round. Meandering pathways, shaded by towering oak and maple trees, guide you through the campus, inviting leisurely strolls and fostering a sense of tranquility amidst the hustle and bustle of academic life.

The buildings themselves are architectural marvels, seamlessly integrating advanced technology with sustainable design. Solar panels and green roofs adorn many structures, reflecting the institution's commitment to environmental stewardship. Large, floor-to-ceiling windows flood the interiors with natural light, creating an open and airy atmosphere conducive to learning and collaboration.

Digital signage and holographic assistants are strategically placed throughout the campus, providing real-time updates on events, schedules, and campus news. These sleek, interactive displays also offer maps and directions, ensuring that visitors and new students can easily navigate their way around. At the heart of the campus, a massive digital mural, created by art students using augmented reality, tells the story of the university's rich history and its vision for the future.

People move about with a sense of purpose, yet there is a palpable feeling of community and connection. Students gather in small groups on the lawns, engaged in animated discussions or quietly studying. Faculty members walk side by side with students, deep in conversation about a recent lecture or research project. Periodically, an administrator joins in the discussion. There is a notable absence of hierarchy; everyone interacts with a sense of mutual respect and camaraderie.

In the central plaza, a diverse group of students is gathered around a series of interactive virtual reality displays, exploring virtual landscapes for their environmental science class. Nearby, a professor conducts a hybrid class, seamlessly integrating in-person students with those attending virtually through a holographic display that projects remote classmates into the physical space.

Interactions are warm and genuine. A student struggling with a difficult problem is quickly surrounded by peers offering assistance. Faculty members are easily approachable, often found sharing coffee with students in the campus café, discussing ideas beyond the classroom setting. There is a strong sense of belonging and mutual support that permeates every aspect of campus life.

This is the College of Tomorrow, a beacon of innovation and inclusivity, where Courageous Leadership for Adaptive Change (CLAC) shapes every facet of its existence. While the campus scene is a captivating one, the true impact and efficacy of the College of Tomorrow lies with operations, which is the catalyst for the culture, climate, and campus vitality. Here's a vivid portrayal of how such an institution operates, humanizes others, pours into the community and the institution itself, supports shared governance, boosts enrollment, fosters partnerships, and leads into a digital future teeming with uncertainty.

Operating With Vision and Agility

At the College of Tomorrow, agile resilience and strategic vision are the twin pillars supporting its operation. Leaders here don't just respond to changes; they anticipate them. For example, when a sudden technological advancement reshapes online education, the CLAC leaders don't scramble. Instead, they seamlessly integrate new tools into their teaching strategies, ensuring faculty and students are not only prepared but excited about the opportunities these changes bring.

Innovation Days are regular events where faculty, staff, and students collaborate to brainstorm and test new ideas. This ensures the university remains at the cutting edge, offering an educational experience that evolves to meet the needs of a dynamic world.

Humanizing Others Through Compassion and Connection

Compassionate connectivity is the bedrock of the College of Tomorrow. Leaders prioritize genuine relationships and ensure every voice is heard. They establish programs like "Campus Voices," monthly forums where everyone, from students to senior faculty, can share their thoughts and concerns directly with the administration. This open communication fosters inclusivity and belonging, making every community member feel valued and respected.

The annual "Global Days" event celebrates the diverse cultures on campus, featuring workshops, panels, and festivities that enhance global competency and mutual respect. These initiatives go beyond mere acknowledgment; they are immersive experiences that bring people together.

Pouring Into Others and the Institution

Authentic empowerment is the heartbeat of this institution. Leaders are deeply committed to personal and professional growth, not just for themselves but for everyone around them. Mentorship programs pair senior faculty and administrators with newer members, fostering a culture of continuous learning.

Financial stewardship is approached with the same innovative spirit. Leaders are entrepreneurial, constantly seeking new partnerships and revenue streams. For example, they might develop corporate partnerships to fund research centers, providing students with cutting-edge resources while securing additional funding for the university. This approach ensures the institution's financial health and aligns with its mission of educational excellence.

Empowering Shared Governance

Shared governance is not just a policy but a practice embedded in the College of Tomorrow's culture. The university operates on the principle that everyone's voice matters and decision-making should be collaborative.

Faculty, staff, and students all have seats at the table through a robust system of committees and councils that influence key policies and strategic directions.

Transparency and accountability are championed through regular town hall meetings and detailed reports on decision-making processes. Multi-stakeholder focus groups are formed to discuss institutional concerns and goals. These measures foster trust and a sense of collective ownership, building a cohesive environment where every member feels empowered and invested in the institution's success.

Boosting Enrollment Through Strategic Initiatives

While the student body is thriving, maintaining a bolster enrollment is a key priority, tackled with a multifaceted strategy. Today's students seek more than just a degree; they want an enriching experience that prepares them for an unpredictable future. The College of Tomorrow excels by offering innovative programs, flexible learning options, and robust support services.

The "Future-Ready Scholarship Program" targets high-achieving students from diverse backgrounds, offering financial support, mentorship, and career guidance. Personalized outreach and virtual tours, coupled with social media campaigns highlighting alumni and current student success stories, attract prospective students by showcasing the vibrant community and opportunities available.

Retention is equally prioritized with dedicated student success centers providing academic support, career counseling, and mental health resources, ensuring students have the tools to thrive.

Fostering Community, Industry, and Academic Partnerships

Promoting partnerships is a cornerstone of the College of Tomorrow's mission. CLAC leaders understand that collaborations with the community, industry, and academia are vital for providing students with practical experiences and ensuring the institution remains relevant.

Industry partnerships offer students internships, co-op programs, and job placements in emerging fields like biotechnology and artificial intelligence. For instance, a partnership with a leading tech company might result in a campus innovation lab where students work on real-world projects alongside industry professionals.

Community engagement is equally important. The university collaborates with local organizations to address social issues and contribute to regional development. The "Community Engagement Program" allows students to work on service projects, gaining valuable skills and experiences while benefiting local communities.

Academic partnerships extend the university's reach. Collaborative research projects with other institutions foster innovation and knowledge sharing, while exchange programs offer students global perspectives, enhancing their educational experience.

Leading Into a Digital Future

As the digital revolution reshapes every aspect of life, the College of Tomorrow leads in preparing students for an uncertain workforce. Digital literacy is a core component of the curriculum, ensuring all students, regardless of their major, are proficient with the latest technological tools and trends.

Online learning platforms provide flexible education options, integrating with on-campus courses to create a hybrid model that maximizes engagement. Virtual reality and augmented reality technologies create immersive learning experiences, from virtual lab simulations to interactive historical explorations.

Recognizing the ever-changing nature of the workforce, the university offers robust career services focused on future-proof skills. Workshops on critical thinking, creativity, and adaptability prepare students to thrive in any professional environment. The "Digital Future Initiative" pairs students with mentors from various industries, exploring potential career paths and developing the skills needed to succeed.

The Impact of CLAC Leadership

Under the guidance of CLAC leaders, the College of Tomorrow transforms into a thriving hub of innovation, inclusivity, and resilience. The institution doesn't just survive challenges; it thrives, setting new standards in education and community engagement. Leaders here are visionaries, nurturers, and catalysts for change, committed to pouring into their people and their institution.

The potential of institutions like the College of Tomorrow, as proposed here, lies in the power of "good" leadership. We believe there is power in the CLAC framework. By embracing agile resilience, strategic vision, principled influence, authentic empowerment, compassionate connectivity, and entrepreneurial financial stewardship, leaders create an environment where every individual can flourish. The campus becomes a place where ideas are born, nurtured, and transformed into realities, setting a benchmark for others to follow.

Wrap Up

As we draw the curtains on this exploration of the College of Tomorrow, this conceptualization highlights the deleterious impact of vampire leadership in academia. Vampire leadership has stifled progress, drained vitality, and obstructed the path to true innovation. These leaders, who prioritize their own interests over the growth and well-being of their institutions, have left behind a legacy of disengagement and stagnation. In stark contrast, the CLAC framework offers a transformative alternative, one that breathes life back into our universities and empowers every member of the academic community.

CLAC is not just a set of principles but a call to action. It urges leaders to be agile and resilient, to possess a strategic vision that extends beyond the present, to influence with integrity, to empower authentically, to connect with compassion, and to steward resources with entrepreneurial acumen. By embracing CLAC, leaders can transform their institutions into dynamic, innovative, and inclusive environments where every individual can thrive.

The Colleges of the Future, guided by CLAC leaders, will not only adapt to the ever-changing educational landscape but will lead the way in shaping it. These institutions will be places where ideas are nurtured, collaboration is fostered, and every voice is heard. They will be vibrant hubs of innovation, inclusivity, and resilience, setting new standards in higher education and beyond.

In urging leaders to consider CLAC, we advocate for a shift from extraction to cultivation, from secrecy to transparency, and from fear to empowerment. The path to creating Colleges of the Future lies in the hands of those willing to lead with courage, adaptability, and a genuine commitment to the well-being of their institutions and communities.

Let us move forward with the vision of a brighter future, where the shadows cast by vampire leadership are dispelled by the light of innovation, integrity, and inclusivity. In this new dawn, our universities can truly become beacons of hope and progress, led by those who pour into their people and institutions, ensuring that they not only survive but thrive in the face of any challenge.

Every student, faculty member, staff personnel, alumnus, industry partner, and community collaborator deserves an institution like the College of Tomorrow. And, we all deserve CLAC leaders.

Discussions and Actions

In Chapter 13, we explored the vision of a "College of Tomorrow" guided by the CLAC framework. This framework emphasizes the principles of Agile

Resilience, Strategic Vision, Principled Influence, Authentic Empowerment, Compassionate Connectivity, and Entrepreneurial Financial Stewardship.

1. *How Can You Implement the CLAC Framework?* Based on the principles of CLAC, conceptualize your own idea of a "College of Tomorrow." How will you ensure that every individual on campus feels valued and indispensable? How will your institution adapt to the changing educational landscape and lead with courage and innovation?
2. *Reflection:*
   - *Imagine the Future:* How do you envision the "College of Tomorrow"? Consider the physical campus, the culture, the operational strategies, and the leadership styles that will define this future institution. Reflect on how these elements can create an environment where everyone feels indispensable and valued.
3. *Leading a Transformative Initiative:* Imagine you are appointed the president of a mid-sized university facing declining enrollment and financial instability. Using the CLAC framework, outline a strategic initiative to transform the university into a thriving "College of Tomorrow."

   Details:

   - *Agile Resilience:* Implement a rapid response plan for immediate challenges and future crises.
   - *Strategic Vision:* Develop a visionary roadmap for the next decade, including new academic programs and partnerships.
   - *Principled Influence:* Establish transparent governance practices and ethical leadership training.
   - *Authentic Empowerment:* Launch initiatives that empower faculty, staff, and students to innovate and lead.
   - *Compassionate Connectivity:* Create programs that enhance community engagement and support diversity.
   - *Entrepreneurial Financial Stewardship:* Introduce sustainable financial practices and diversify revenue streams through partnerships and innovation.

AFTERWORD: THE FINAL STAKE

Patrice W. Glenn Jones
Alabama State University, USA

As we close this exploration through vampire leadership, it's clear that this form of toxic leadership has left its mark—a bite, if you will—on the very soul of our educational institutions. Much like the cinematic encounters with Dracula in his dark castle or the eerie moments when Lestat prowls the night, these tales of power gone awry serve as cautionary tales for our time. The stakes are high, and it's time to bring out the metaphorical garlic and sunlight.

Remember the chilling scene in *Nosferatu*, where the count's shadow creeps up the staircase, a silent yet palpable menace? Or perhaps the more contemporary horror in *Blade*, where the hidden vampire elite pulls the strings of human society from the shadows? These narratives are not far removed from the experiences of many within the ivory towers. Vampire leadership, with its insidious influence and draining effects, has cast a long shadow over our hallowed institutions, leaving them anemic and gasping for fresh blood—innovation, empowerment, and genuine human connection.

It's time to flip the script.

Enter the Courageous Leadership for Adaptive Change (CLAC) framework. If Greenleaf's servant leadership was the whisper of transformation, then CLAC is the resounding call to arms, urging leaders at all levels to reclaim the night and turn our academic institutions into vibrant communities of learning and growth. While vampire leaders can drain to the point of individual and organizational mortality, CLAC leaders nurture and create opportunity and empowerment for personal and institutional growth.

Imagine for a moment, the sun-drenched finale of a vampire saga—where the darkness is vanquished, and the world is bathed in light. This is the vision CLAC offers. It proposes a renaissance, where leaders are agile, visionary, principled, authentic, compassionate, and entrepreneurial. This is a call not merely to survive but to thrive.

Our universities need leaders who are more Van Helsing than Dracula, more Buffy than Spike. These are leaders who confront challenges head-on, wielding the cross of integrity and the holy water of empathy. They turn the once-shadowy corners of governance into well-lit spaces of collaboration and shared purpose.

For instance, think of the iconic scene in *Interview with the Vampire*, where Louis, weary of the ceaseless night, seeks the warmth of the sun. Like Louis, our institutions yearn for the dawn, a break from the stifling grip of vampire leadership. CLAC provides the tools to usher in this new era. By fostering environments where every stakeholder—students, faculty, staff, and administrators—feels valued and heard, we can finally banish the vampiric tendencies that have long plagued our academies.

This transformation requires boldness and a collective will. To every leader reading this, at every level: the time for change is now. Whether you are a department chair, a dean, a university president, or an emerging leader, you hold the power to make a difference. Embrace the principles of CLAC and champion the cause of renewal and innovation. It's time to drive the final stake through the heart of vampire leadership and herald a new dawn for higher education.

In the spirit of our journey, let us remember that even the most fearsome vampire stories end with hope—with the monster vanquished and the dawn breaking. Let's channel that spirit and become the heroes our institutions need. After all, the power to create the Colleges of the Future lies not in the shadows, but in the light we bring to our leadership.

Stake in hand, onward we go.

REFERENCES

Ali, A., Tariq, H., & Wang, Y. (2023). Finding the silver lining: Why and when abusive supervision improves the objective service performance of abused employees. *Asia Pacific Journal of Management.* https://doi.org/10.1007/s10490-023-09927-z

Argyris, C., & Schon, D. (1974). *Theory in practice: Increasing professional effectiveness.* Jossey Bass.

Argyris, C., & Schon, D. A. (1976). Theory in practice: Increasing professional effectiveness. *Contemporary Sociology, 5*(2), 197.

Argyris, C., & Schon, D. A. (1992). *Theory in practice: Increasing professional effectiveness.* John Wiley & Sons.

Aryee, S., Chen, Z. X., Sun, L. Y., & Debrah, Y. A. (2007). Antecedents and outcomes of abusive supervision: Test of a trickle-down model. *Journal of Applied Psychology, 92*(1), 191–201.

Asch, S. E. (1956). Studies of independence and conformity: I. A minority of one against a unanimous majority. *Psychological Monographs: General and Applied, 70*(9), 1–70. https://doi.org/10.1037/h0093718

Avolio, B. J., Sosik, J. J., Kahai, S. S., & Baker, B. (2014). E-leadership: Re-examining transformations in leadership source and transmission. *The Leadership Quarterly, 25*(1), 105–131.

Babad, E. (1995). The "teacher's pet" phenomenon, students' perceptions of teachers' differential behavior, and students' morale. *Journal of Educational Psychology, 87*(3), 361.

Bakker, A. B., Demerouti, E., & Verbeke, W. (2004). Using the job demands-resources model to predict burnout and performance. *Human Resource Management, 43*(1), 83–104.

Bandura, A. (1977). Self-efficacy: Toward a unifying theory of behavioral change. *Psychological Review, 84*(2), 191.

Bandura, A. (1986). *Social foundations of thought and action.* Prentice-Hall, Inc.

Bennis, W. G. (1989). *On becoming a leader.* Addison-Wesley.

Bennis, W. G. (2000). *Managing people is like herding cats.* Executive Excellence Publishing.

Bies, R. J., & Moag, J. F. (1986). *Interactional justice: Communication criteria of fairness* (R. J. Lewicki, B. H. Sheppard, & M. H. Bazerman, Eds., Vol. 1, pp. 43–55). JAI Press.

Braun, S., Peus, C., Weisweiler, S., & Frey, D. (2013). Transformational leadership, job satisfaction, and team performance: A multilevel mediation model of trust. *The Leadership Quarterly, 24*(1), 270–283.

Burns, J. M. (1978). *Leadership.* Harper & Row.

Burns, J. M. (2012). *Leadership.* Open Road Media.

Carlson, D. S., Ferguson, M., Perrewé, P. L., & Whitten, D. (2011). The fallout from abusive supervision: An examination of subordinates and their partners. *Personnel Psychology, 64*(4), 937–961.

Chun, E., & Evans, A. (2023). *The academic department chair as transformative diversity leader.* https://www.cupahr.org/hew/files/HEWorkplace-Vol7No2-ICE.pdf

Eccles, J., Wigfield, A., Harold, R. D., & Blumenfeld, P. (1993). Age and gender differences in children's self-and task perceptions during elementary school. *Child Development, 64*(3), 830–847.

Eden, D. (1992). Leadership and expectations: Pygmalion effects and other self-fulfilling prophecies in organizations. *The Leadership Quarterly, 3*(4), 271–305.

Feldman, D. C. (1984). The development and enforcement of group norms. *Academy of Management Review, 9*(1), 47–53.

Fischer, T., Tian, A. W., Lee, A., & Hughes, D. J. (2021). Abusive supervision: A systematic review and fundamental rethink. *The Leadership Quarterly, 32*(6), 101540.

Gazzola, V., Rizzolatti, G., Wicker, B., & Keysers, C. (2007). The anthropomorphic brain: The mirror neuron system responds to human and robotic actions. *NeuroImage, 35*(4), 1674–1684.

Hallinger, P., & Heck, R. H. (1996). The principal's role in school effectiveness: An assessment of methodological progress, 1980–1995. In *International handbook of educational leadership and administration: Part1–2* (pp. 723–783). Springer Netherlands.

Hashimy, S. Q., Jahromi, A., Hamza, M., Naaz, I., Nyamwero, N. B., & HT, B. (2023). Nurturing leadership and capacity building for success: Empowering growth. *International Journal of Rehabilitation & Special Education, 3*(2).

Hattie, J., & Timperley, H. (2007). The power of feedback. *Review of Educational Research, 77*(1), 81–112.

Hecht, I., Higgerson, M., Gmelch, W., & Tucker, A. (1999). *The department chair as academic leader.* Oryx Press.

Jones, P. W. (2016). Nurturing leadership: A potential leadership approach to influence achievement among Black male students. In *NAAAS Conference Proceedings* (p. 503). National Association of African American Studies.

Jones, P. W. (2017). *Sense of community and hope: An exploration among leaders at African American high schools.* Doctoral dissertation. Florida Agricultural and Mechanical University.

Jussim, L., & Harber, K. D. (2005). Teacher expectations and self-fulfilling prophecies: Knowns and unknowns, resolved and unresolved controversies. *Personality and Social Psychology Review, 9*(2), 131–155.

Kellerman, B. (2004). *Bad leadership: What it is, how it happens, why it matters.* Harvard Business School Press.

Kiesler, C. A., & Kiesler, S. B. (1969). *Conformity.* Addison-Wesley Publications.

Koopman, J., Lanaj, K., & Scott, B. A. (2016). Integrating the bright and dark sides of OCB: A daily investigation of the benefits and costs of helping others. *Academy of Management Journal, 59*(2), 414–435.

Kouzes, J., & Posner, B. Z. (2017). *The leadership challenge: How to make extraordinary things happen in organizations*. Wiley.

Leithwood, K., & Jantzi, D. (2008). Linking leadership to student learning: The contributions of leader efficacy. *Educational Administration Quarterly, 44*(4), 496–528.

Liang, L. H., Lian, H., Brown, D. J., Ferris, D. L., Hanig, S., & Keeping, L. M. (2016). Why are abusive supervisors abusive? A dual-system self-control model. *Academy of Management Journal, 59*(4), 1385–1406.

Lipman-Blumen, J. (2004). *The allure of toxic leaders: Why we follow destructive bosses and corrupt politicians – and how we can survive them*. Oxford University Press.

Mackey, J. D., Frieder, R. E., Brees, J. R., & Martinko, M. J. (2017). Abusive supervision: A meta-analysis and empirical review. *Journal of Management, 43*(6), 1940–1965.

Marshall, J. D., Aguinis, H., & Beltran, J. R. (2024). Theories of performance: A review and integration. *The Academy of Management Annals, 18*(2), 600–625.

Mawritz, M. B., Mayer, D. M., Hoobler, J. M., Wayne, S. J., & Marinova, S. V. (2012). A trickle-down model of abusive supervision. *Personnel Psychology, 65*(2), 325–357.

Muñoz, A. J., Pankake, A. M., Mills, S., & Simonsson, M. (2018). Nurturing leadership: Equitable mentoring for the superintendency. *International Journal of Leadership in Education, 21*(3), 284–292.

Padilla, A., Hogan, R., & Kaiser, R. (2007). The toxic triangle: Destructive leaders, susceptible followers, and conducive environments. *The Leadership Quarterly, 18*, 176-194.

Picca, L. H., & Feagin, J. R. (2007). *Two-faced racism: Whites in the backstage and frontstage*. Routledge/Taylor & Francis Group.

Rizzolatti, G., & Craighero, L. (2004). The mirror-neuron system. *Annual Review of Neuroscience, 27*, 169–192.

Rosenberg, B. (2024). *The impossible college presidency*. The Chronicle of Higher Education.

Rosenholtz, S. J., & Simpson, C. (1984). The formation of ability conceptions: Developmental trend or social construction? *Review of Educational Research, 54*(1), 31–63.

Rosenthal, R., & Jacobson, L. (1968). Pygmalion in the classroom. *The Urban Review, 3*(1), 16–20.

Rotundo, M., & Sackett, P. R. (2002). The relative importance of task, citizenship, and counterproductive performance to global ratings of job performance: A policy-capturing approach. *Journal of Applied Psychology, 87*(1), 66–80.

Seligman, A. B. (1998). Trust and sociability: On the limits of confidence and role expectations. *The American Journal of Economics and Sociology, 57*(4), 391–404.

Singer, T. (2006). The neuronal basis and ontogeny of empathy and mind reading: Review of literature and implications for future research. *Neuroscience & Biobehavioral Reviews, 30*(6), 855–863.

Tepper, B. J. (2000). Consequences of abusive supervision. *Academy of Management Journal, 43*(2), 178–190.

Van Wart, M., Rahman, S., & Mazumdar, T. (2021). The dark side of resilient leaders: Vampire leadership. *Transylvanian Review of Administrative Sciences, 17*(SI), 144–165.

Vaughan, G., & Hogg, M. A. (2005). *Introduction to social psychology*. Pearson Education Australia.

Whitman, M. V., Halbesleben, J. R. B., & Holmes IV, O. (2014). Abusive supervision and feedback avoidance: The mediating role of emotional exhaustion. *Journal of Organizational Behavior, 35*, 38–53.

Wicker, M. (1996). *Toxic leaders: When organizations go bad.* Praeger.

Williams, I., Glenn, P., & Wider, F. (2008). Nurtured advising. *Academic Advising Today.* https://www.nacada.ksu.edu/Portals/0/ePub/documents/31-1.pdf